POWER PERSUASION

6 STRATEGIES TO INSTANTLY INFLUENCE & HYPNOTIZE BOTH ONLINE AND OFFLINE

Confessions of a hypnotist, marketer and ex door to door salesman

MUNEER AL BUSAIDI

Get my FREE guide – 11 Hypnotic Power words of Persuasion: Discover hot words used by hypnotists that you can start using in the next 47 minutes to make your everyday communication more persuasive

http://www.muneer.com/powerwords/

ENDORSEMENTS AND ACCOLADES

"Muneer is one of those people who will only ever have a positive impact on others, hence why he has become not only a great friend of mine but part of my family. "My brother from another Mother" Having been with Muneer during both highs and lows in his life (and mine), I have only ever known him to have a positive impact on those around him. With clear views on how to progress and improve in any given situation, Muneer would be the one person you would want by your side in a difficult situation.

A Marketing Expert, Global Comedian, Hypnosis legend, and an Inspiration to not only tens if not hundreds of thousands of people globally, but to those closest to him. Muneer a blessing to us all"

Richard Long,
Founder & CEO Jefferson Wolfe
www.jeffersonwolfe.com

""I registered and attended one of Muneer's programs "The Client creation formula" a program that helped me get started on social media, choose blog topics, launch a website that performs better than the industry average, and identify and leverage valuable assets. Through Muneer's support, I am finding and connecting to worlds of knowledge I otherwise wouldn't know about and I couldn't have gotten to where I am without Muneer. He gave me the confidence and drive to organize, build and plan my "Health Recovery and Body shape system". I will be forever grateful for his knowledge and support that was easily and effortlessly implemented."

Dr Hanan Selim,
Founder of HCBHconsultancy

(Hanan Consultancy for better health)* Dr Hanan lost 28kgs and transformed her health and life, with Muneer's help she now transforms the lives of others through her system
www.drhananselim.com

"Most people define success by what they have done or what they have in their lives. Muneer measures success by how much of a difference he has made to someone else's life. Whether it is for a colleague at work, people he is coaching or a friend he knows, Muneer's goal is to have a positive effect on the people around him in his life and he achieves this goal very well!"

Mohammed Loch,
President & CEO DMS Global, Regional Director Manufacturing Enterprise Solutions Association (MESA), Director Bilateral US-Arab Chamber of Commerce, Partner & Exec Director – The Choice to change foundation

"Muneer is the Master of persuasion . He is the one person I can trust to teach people how to influence and take charge of their life. A must read!!"

Arfeen Khan,
Peak Performance Strategist
ArfeenKhan.com

"Muneer is one of those rare individuals that has a vision and way of thinking that many instructors can't achieve, he has created many beneficial and relatable courses and content that is delivered in a style that is absolutely terrific! Especially the humor and the ability to drive a point home where the new knowledge becomes second nature, I have taken his courses and I'm very glad I did, because I have implemented all of his teachings into my business and mindset and am blessed to say that I used to be a charity case and now I can donate to charities. "

Rick Sharif,
CEO Arkham Creative
ArkhamCreative.com

"Muneer is extremely knowledgable and passionate about the mind sciences. He has taken NLP and Hypnosis to another level. Muneer will go wherever it takes to learn cutting edge techniques that give him the edge. He is passionate about helping others and making a difference. His unique and funny style makes him a pleasure to listen to"

Rita Baki,
Managing partner The Change Associates
http://www.changeassociates.ae/

"Muneer is a person who not only knows his stuff but delivers it in a unique and entertaining way. I have big expectations for him stepping onto the global scene, smashing stereotypes and delivering awesome content that will help us all"

Ruben West
Speaker, Author, Success Coach & Trainer
www.Rubenwest360.com

Muneer has this amazing ability to make everyone around him smile. He has an incredible way of connecting with people from all walks of life, all ages and all backgrounds. When you meet him, you feel like you have known him your whole life. I have been fortunate enough to have known

Muneer for over 16 years and I would not be where I am today, if it wasn't for him. He is someone that leaves a positive impression on everyone he meets and genuinely is in this- to help others. He knows first hand, how drive and positive motivation, can change your life. He can and will help so many people and I feel so lucky to have him in my life.

Bianca Skinner
Founder Retro & Magic Apparels

Acknowledgements:

First and foremost, I would like to thank God for allowing me to get to a stage in my life where I have had the courage to pursue all my dreams and move beyond any self doubt.

I would like to thank my wife Aneta for her support, and my daughter Sara who always looks up to me, mainly because she is currently much shorter than me. However, her presence has given me such a drive and determination to ensure that when she grows up she continues to do so.

I would like to thank my parents for all the opportunities that they have strived to provide me with, all of which have shaped me into the person I am today, as well as my close family: Nabs, Salha, Sabrina, Narmeen and Yarub for all the laughter and setting the bars high for me to live up to.

My best friend Rick for helping me throughout the years with so many of my crazy ideas, and allowing me to push him which in turn pushed myself.

To all the coaches that I have had over the years who played a huge part in shaping this journey, from my great friend Richard Long, my first ever sales teacher, who taught an Omani boy to suit up and get to the top in London.

To Arfeen Khan who has coached me, pushed me to write this book and pushed me to go further than ever before.

I also want to thank the teachers who I have had the opportunity to meet and learn so much from, especially Richard Bandler who subconsciously rewired me to want and achieve more while learning NLP from him.

I would also like to acknowledge some of the people that have made a big difference in my life, though I have not yet had the pleasure of meeting them: Anthony Robbins, whose CD's have shaped my life for so many years; Igor Ledochovski, whose hypnosis training lessons have pushed me to become a better hypnotist and persuader; and Dr Robert Cialdini, whose countless experiments in the field allowed me to add some data to all my theories.

I want to thank Emile and Rita for their huge support in allowing me to pursue my dreams.

I would like to give a huge thanks to Tony Sidgwick who helped a novice writer create a book worthy of being read by editing my book and to Bhavna Patel who proof read the finished version and pushed me to make it just a little better.

For all my friends and family who are too many to mention here (especially the family... have you ever met an Arab family?), I love you all and am blessed to have you all in my life.

WHY DID I WRITE THIS BOOK?

I wrote this book because I have come across too many people who believe that influence, persuasion and charisma are something that a person must be born with.

This is simply not the case - these are skills that can be learned. While I do not claim to be the world's leading expert on influence and persuasion, as there are without doubt those out there with more knowledge of the field than me, through learning the secrets I will be sharing with you in this book I went from the bullied kid at school to being nicknamed the 'master of persuasion'.

If someone as unpopular as myself (we are talking about eight years of being socially awkward and unpopular) can learn to become a 'master of persuasion', I believe that anybody can do it.

Apart from my experience in sales, NLP, marketing and hypnosis, I've travelled the world learning from the best out there, and have read many many books on influence, persuasion and the reasons people do what they do.

While I learned from all of them, I didn't find one singular place that alone accurately represented all of my experience and research, and none that did so in an entertaining way.

After all, a major part of charisma is not taking yourself too seriously, while having great intentions for others. I therefore set out to create a book that was entertaining to read, taught you the best of what is out there, and provided a few laughs along the way, because when people have fun, learning gets done!

WHY SHOULD YOU READ THIS BOOK

Stated simply, this book will help you to get more people to do what you want them to, whether it's to buy your product, or agree with your decisions, or even just turn up to your dinner party.

Everyone persuades or is persuaded every single day. Persuasion doesn't necessarily have to relate to sales, it is present in all the adverts we see on a daily basis and in simple things we do, such as asking a friend to join you or give you something.

This book outlines the reasons why people do what they do, and how understanding this will allow you to mold interactions to your advantage. It's backed by a lot of research carried out by various successful people over the past few decades.

This book can be used by everyone - from sales people and marketers, to parents, negotiators, employers, employees, husbands, wives, or even people looking for husbands or wives!

People will often find that it applies to many of the different roles that they play in life. You may have a team reporting to you, as well as a boss you report to (guys, I'm referring to the workplace here, not your wife!). You may be an educator, or coach a sports team in your spare time.

However, many of you may also have a spouse and children, parents and places you shop, or on the odd occasion, you may need to sell something, like a car or a house. You can save and make crazy money in those certain big transactions using the techniques you'll find in this book.

Whatever your situation in life, I believe that this book will benefit you in many ways, once you uncover the secrets and apply them in your everyday life.

TABLE OF CONTENTS

How a man from Oman went from bullied to a Master of Persuasion

Before you panic, don't worry – this isn't a biography. However, I feel it's important to give you a little background about myself in order to give you an understanding of how I know this subject inside-out, whilst also demonstrating that this is a skill that anyone can learn.

So please bear with me if this begins to seem like a chapter about how awesome I am (even though I totally am...). It is intended to show you why I have personally earned the right to write about this subject, versus someone else that is simply regurgitating information.

So why keep reading?

Have you ever noticed that there are people in life that have opinions about everything? Perhaps you may even know someone who feels the need to share them with you regularly (cough, Auntie Fatima, cough...).

For example: I have myself invested in a few properties, and when I was buying my second property in the UAE (where I live), I had someone come up to me talking about how it was a bad investment, and the market was down, and he recommended that I invest in Brazil instead. The crazy thing is that this guy had never touched an investment in his life!

Instead I took on Warren Buffet's advice, which was simply:

"When people are fearful be greedy; when people are greedy be fearful."

The reason that I tell you this story is because it's a confusing reality that advice is everywhere. The question is, whose advice are YOU taking? Never ask an obese person how to lose weight, a street sweeper how to be rich, or a pink flamingo how to blend into its surroundings... principally because flamingos don't speak English.

If you want to get somewhere you have never been, asking someone that has never been there for directions can potentially get you lost (don't be that person who says "But what if they have a map?" – nobody likes that person... don't do it!).

So where do I fit in? I am someone that understands both sides of the coin – from the non-influential and unpopular place right up to what you need to learn to become a persuasion champion.

People often assume that "charisma", "charm" and the ability to persuade or sell is a natural ability or agene that you are born with. You often hear the naysayers go, "It's easy for him to say... he doesn't know what it's like to be shy, awkward, a bad conversationalist etc."

I, however, can claim that I know exactly what it's like to be shy, unpopular and afraid of rejection. I was arguably the textbook definition of awkward for over eight years of my life. I can relate to more of the following statements than most:

- I was bullied and made fun of.
- I was self-conscious and always wondering what people would think of me.
- I was unpopular with everyone my age (especially the girls who I so desperately wanted to be popular with!).
- I was extremely awkward in social contexts.
- I found it difficult to meet anyone new and even when I did I had no idea what to say to people.
- I couldn't convince myself that I was good enough, let alone convince others to agree with anything I said.

Let me paint you a little picture of how my teenage years went – I had terrible eyesight, was scrawny and extremely unconfident. My eyeglass prescription was -6, which is heavy! As a result I used to have to wear coke bottles for glasses; to give you an idea of how strong they were, if a normal person put them on they could probably see back in time!

We have all grown up in different environments, but I can tell you one universal thing: kids don't always understand the concept of respecting the feelings of others... Indeed, for me it was quite the opposite: I suffered quite a number of years of being pushed around by the guys, laughed at by the girls and empathised with by no-one.

If I'd had an imaginary friend, he would've pretended that he didn't know me when others were around!

However, from time-to-time in everyone's life comes those pivotal moments that can dramatically alter the direction that your life is heading in – it could be the day you pick up a book, the day something forces you to change or the day you decide enough is enough.

Well, when I was about 16 years-old my life began to take a new direction, and it all started when one of the bullies had pushed me a little too far one day...

I was being made fun of once again, but on that day the bully decided to condescendingly pat my face a couple of times, and for some reason something in me just snapped at that moment, and without thinking I just lashed out.

I'd had enough, I had grown, and I had decided to stand up for myself. I decided it was time to take a stand once and for all, and so, at this turning point in my life in what was one of the biggest fights I've ever been in, I threw this punch and...

... I lost the fight miserably!

However, while I may have lost the physical battle on the day, I had won an even more important one - the battle for my self-respect, and the end of an era in which I was bullied. You see, bullies like easy targets, and once I had stood up for myself and there was a risk I would do it again, they decided to just leave me alone.

And so I'd reached a point where I wasn't popular, but I wasn't necessarily unpopular either – I was just 'there'.

Now the truth is, I had always wanted to be well-liked - my father would walk around town and everyone would know him and greet him warmly, and I had cousins that were very popular, yet I knew that I was the opposite.

So I decided to start reading a little bit, just out of curiosity. I read books like *How to Win Friends and Influence People*, and books of jokes because I knew that people liked to hear jokes. I didn't exactly have a strategy – I was just short on friends and long on time.

I decided to start working a little on my appearance too, because I learned that although people say, "you shouldn't judge a book by its cover", the blunt truth is that people often do select a book based on the cover before they can make a judgement on the book's contents. First impressions are often the most important that you make on people!

So, I started working out a little, and also started wearing contact lenses (I later also had laser eye surgery, which was well worth it!). I did all this with no real expectations, just curiosity… and because I had nothing better to do.

Now, if you have ever experienced significant weight change, then you will understand that both you and the people around you don't really notice anything until one day you're so far from what you were that it just shocks you.

Because I started my journey of transformation around the people that hadn't liked me, I didn't see how far my skills had come until I went to university a couple of years later. When I arrived, I somehow became one of the most popular people at my whole university. I was asked to do everything and be in everything, from DJing to radio shows, and received invitations to all the various society functions. I was even elected to head up the international student committee.

I didn't even know how to explain it myself, but I was too busy enjoying it to think about it too much. No-one knew about my past, and to be honest, I am ashamed that at the time I even tried to hide it. I got rid of every picture and piece of evidence of my childhood from the age of 10 to 18. What I did know, however, is that my interest in connection, influence and persuasion had paid off.

After university, I applied for many different roles, but getting your first job is always tough. What made it tougher was that I had studied engineering, and the biggest thing I'd learned is that engineering was the last thing I wanted to do!

Whilst job hunting, I stumbled across an opportunity which led to a role in door-to-door sales. I acknowledge that no-one ever goes to a great university with the aim of becoming a door-to-door salesman. In fact, it's nobody's first choice! I've never spoken at a school and heard kids saying, "When I grow up, I want to walk the streets in English weather knocking on doors for commission!"

The truth, however, it that I was extremely attracted to the role purely for the reason that it was the ultimate experience in pure persuasion – the very definition of influence and persuasion education.

Everything about that role was pure persuasion genius. From the way they advertised to entice new prospects to the job (often referred to as 'direct marketing executive' roles), to how they create excitement within people to join the role on their own accord, it was amazing how they would turn a person from wondering if this was something they should do to hoping they were selected to fill the role.

What excited me the most, though, was that the people who were there and the ones who were training me were some of the most positive and charismatic people I had ever met. And... they had a 'system'. The system that I teach you in this book has evolved from that very system I learned in those days.

The difference between those old sales techniques and the sophisticated methods I teach you today is that I have modified it all based on all my research into many other systems, and I have incorporated tried-and-tested NLP and hypnotic patterns into the principles while ensuring that everything that applies does so for both the digital and real world.

The origins of these principles were based on a system that I initially learned and thereafter taught, and were the basis for creating some of the top door-to-door salespeople in the whole of the UK.

I wouldn't say I was the fastest learner, but I was super keen, and I had a passion for learning how to relate to people instantly and getting people to do what I wanted. I had spent so many years feeling helpless that this felt like learning a super power.

After just a few months, I rose to become one of the top salespeople in the whole of the UK, a field of many thousands of people – no small feat for an Omani boy living so far from home. When salespeople do well in the field, they are then asked to train others, and you are slowly given a team to build which can increase your income.

After making a few mistakes with my first few trainees, I realized that the trick to building a team that constantly performs is to develop a system that works for every person, every time. The company had its own system, and I just had to build on that slightly to go further than the others. So, I developed a system that allowed me to train people into becoming some of the top salespeople in the country as well.

It took some trial and error, and I had trained people who became exceptional at sales. Then came a day that I had trained a person who became the number one salesperson in the UK just one week after joining the company. This is when I knew that I had an amazing system that anyone could use, and I could teach anyone to be the best! I fell in love with systems because they are transferable, while people are not.

I understood that for me to have a successful team, everyone had to do well, and for everyone to do well in my team, I needed a strong system –

it was not about me being strong, it was about my system being strong.

After two years in the field of door-to-door sales, I moved on to bigger and better things:

* I worked for an airline conducting corporate sales in South Africa, combining my love of travel with my love of influence and persuasion. I learned here the differences between a consumer selling environment and a corporate selling environment.

* Following this I moved to Bahrain and into a marketing role. Although marketing contained persuasion, I was initially dissatisfied with the role, and I started looking for ways to increase my income.

* I started an online business – this was a new challenge because when I did door to door sales, I had a product that applied to every home, and when I worked in corporate sales, I was told which businesses my product applied to and I knew where to go.

When I created my online business, I realized that I could not just promote to every person I saw; it was a specific product that certain people would be interested in, though not everyone. I decided that I needed to learn how to work smarter and not harder, and so started learning digital marketing; essentially how to find people online who are looking for what you have.

If you ever want to be very good at something very quickly, put your own money on the line when you don't have much of it! Trust me: investing in yourself makes you get efficient real quick – you don't want to spend a spare dime that could have gone towards buying food or possibly even socks (socks have always been a very holy item for me... and I don't mean in the religious sense!).

I had to learn quickly how to optimize my ads and apply influence and persuasion to an online and digital world. This was also at a time in the Middle East where many businesses hadn't even heard of online marketing.

I soon found that the systems that I had learned previously for influence and persuasion still applied, though they needed to be adjusted slightly because of the format. I also learned new elements that I had not been aware of before.

Many online marketers teach you how to build an online business – sales people teach how to sell offline. I had to develop my own system to combine the two using the most effective elements of prospecting online and converting offline.

After two years of promoting my business and gaining customers that spanned a number of countries in the Middle East and Africa, all of a sudden, out of the blue, the product was discontinued.

This was a huge blow for me – Two years of my life building a business. TWO YEARS!

I am a positive person and I worked hard to find the positive spins for myself, but believe me it was tough... I told myself: "This will make my success story even more compelling!" And, "I have learned things that are extremely valuable." Et cetera, et cetera.

Fortunately, the next stage appeared almost instantly. It's important to remember at this point that even if someone takes an opportunity away from you, they can never take the skills that you have gained.

Almost immediately after my setback, I was headhunted to head up the digital marketing for a global brand, and then headhunted again to do it for another even bigger global brand. I held a senior position and had gained corporate success, applying my knowledge online for these major brands.

There was a catch though: After spending some time initially building and setting things up while learning the ins and outs of the role, it quickly became a fairly monotonous task, because I realised that I was no longer:

-Learning new things any more,

-Actually helping people better their lives,

-Subjected to new and cutting-edge influence and persuasion techniques.

This realisation led me down the path of starting to learn NLP and hypnosis. After all, I had learned and applied so much influence and persuasion, yet I had never conducted a deep study into the science of human behavior. At the time Dr Richard Bandler, the co-creator of NLP, happened to be teaching the subject, so I felt that I should go and learn from the best.

This opened my eyes to a whole new level of persuasion and influence at a subconscious level. The ability to make lifelong changes in an instant felt insanely powerful. As an example, I learned to cure phobias in 10 minutes. Lifelong phobias! At the time I was terrified of snakes – growing up I wasn't even able to look at a snake on TV. Toy snakes used to terrify me.

Then I went to this seminar, and was taught how to cure a phobia. The next thing I knew, we were separated into groups to test our learning. There was the 'snake' group, the 'spider' group, the 'heights' group, the 'claustrophobia' group and the 'needle' group.

So there I was, extremely nervous as I was told that in 12 minutes I would be asked to hold a snake, and I was wondering, "Can I do this?" We'd learned the steps to the technique *in theory*, but we had not yet practiced the technique. I was paired with a woman who was actually crying her eyes out, which didn't help the fact that I was probably close to crying myself...

Anyhow, we composed ourselves enough to do the exercises, and within 15 minutes we were both standing there with snakes on our shoulders, and the hugest smiles on our faces because of the breakthrough we had achieved.

That moment was pivotal for me, because it was then that I truly realized how powerful the subconscious mind could be in changing our long-term beliefs and behaviors, whereas previously in that situation I would have had to just change my pants...

This newfound field re-ignited my passion for learning, discovering and helping people. I started travelling the world to learn from many of the best out there about the field of influencing the subconscious mind. I studied, hypnosis, NLP, hypnotherapy, conversational hypnosis, mind-bending language, instant inductions, street hypnosis performances and more.

After studying so much and learning from the best, and reading so many influence and persuasion books, I started to reach a point where I would read things and notice that people would either miss things out or get things wrong, and I slowly began to realise that I too could contribute so much to this field.

Which brings me to this point in which I decided to write a book.

So, to this end, I had to get to a point where I felt this information was really necessary for me to share with the world, because to be perfectly honest, I am usually too lazy to write out messages on Whatsapp, let alone write a whole book. I am 'that guy' who prefers to send those audio notes that people get annoyed with because you can't exactly check them out if you are in a meeting.

If I could have, I would have said, "Ok, you want to learn the art and science of influence and persuasion then you need to: Read this, read that, watch this, go travel here and do this course, research this, etc."

Even thinking about going back and doing all those courses again makes me want to cry. So, after some encouragement, I have decided to write a book and combine all my years of research, experience and learning into one condensed volume.

Come to think of it, maybe I didn't have to write the whole of this chapter – those last few paragraphs pretty much summarise it all... although that's probably like saying the *Lord of the Rings* trilogy is about a short guy that takes a very long walk to throw a ring in some fire.

Whatever, it's my book, so I'm going to do it my way – also known as 'The Awesome Way'.

"My way" might not be the most conventional – I use jokes, ALL of which are funny of course (even if just to me...), tell stories and make fun of the situation and myself. If you are looking for a textbook, then this isn't it.

Overall I want you to enjoy this book as an experience and have fun – because when people have fun... learning gets done!

A QUICK WORD ON HYPNOSIS AND WHAT IT IS

I have always had a fascination with hypnosis, though I understand the misconceptions many people have about hypnosis because I myself had them once upon a time. However after learning the actual science behind hypnosis and NLP, I learned that it is just a way to present information to the mind in a way that is more beneficial and in line with how the brain naturally thinks (allowing it to sink in more easily).

Hypnosis is ultimately a combination of two things:

1. A trance state.
2. Guiding the mind in a particular direction.

Let's start with the trance state.

A trance is actually a very naturally occurring state that most of us experience all the time, often daily. It's a state of focused attention, in which it is not pondering a hundred things simultaneously. Examples of this are:

- When we watch a film we focus all of our attention on the story, getting completely absorbed and in a state of suspended disbelief - we don't consider anything else in the room.
- Athletes get into 'the zone' when they perform their sport – they are not thinking about going to the supermarket, or yesterday's events, etc.
- A musician who is really into playing his music is 'in the flow'.
- An accountant who is buried in the numbers.
- Yoga enthusiasts meditate to "clear their mind" and focus on relaxation.

A trance state is useful because we have more of our brain's resources available to us. Our brain is singularly focused on something. People assume that hypnosis needs to be conducted on someone whilst their eyes are closed. The reality is hypnotists like this because it helps people focus, though it isn't exactly necessary.

A hypnotist just combines a trance state with a direction for your mind to go in:

- Hypnotherapy can direct your mind and resources to solving an outcome and making deep habit changes that a person *already wants to make*.
- A stage show just directs this focused state of attention to getting a person *who volunteers* into a form of deeply immersed roleplaying. The key word is 'volunteers'.

A stage show is great in showing people what the mind is capable of. However, it is important to realize that there are theatrics in a stage show, and stage hypnotists are very selective in order to pick only people whose minds are more open to roleplaying. Roleplaying, a naturally occurring activity that many people do in their everyday lives – think of the man who plays the stern boss at work in front of his employees but the playful clown at home with his children, or the lady who's a fitness guru on social media but a messy slob in private! We all wear different hats each day, and stage hypnotists simply pick out this ability for entertainment.

This process in a hypnosis show brings about two major misconceptions:

1. That some people are not hypnotizable: Just because a mind may not be open to role play doesn't mean they can't be hypnotized – it's just that they won't be fun to watch on a stage since they are less animated.
2. Hypnosis makes you do things that you don't want to do: Consider this – are there people in real life who like to role play and pretend they are people or things they are not? Or perhaps you or someone you know has pretended to be angry and really got into character. A hypnosis show takes this naturally occurring phenomenon with animated people and, with their permission, amplifies it to another level by giving them all the resources of their subconscious mind. By being selective and finding these

people in a show, it gives the illusion that the hypnotist has complete control over a person. However, a volunteer and their subconscious mind *gave* the hypnotist permission to put them into a state of role-play.

No one can make you do something you don't want to do. People say no to things under hypnosis that are against their morals, beliefs and ethics all the time. People that don't really want to quit smoking and do hypnotherapy are not likely to quit, which is why I won't try to help someone who was sent by a parent or wife/husband, unless they really want it themselves.

Believe me, I have tried to get my wife to do all kinds of things without success... not everything works!

The reason I talk about incorporating hypnosis theory into persuasion is because hypnosis is the science of making your suggestions a whole lot more persuasive by using principles and language that the subconscious mind reacts to. Your mind is made up two parts – your conscious and your subconscious, and the subconscious mind constitutes 90% of the total! Your emotions, memories, habits and automatic processes are all stored here. Your conscious mind is 10% of your brain – this is the thinking part. When you first learn to drive a car it's a conscious process, and over time it becomes a subconscious process – you don't have to consciously think about doing it, it becomes habit!

Your subconscious is much more powerful, because it is your 'autopilot' and controls 90% of your mind's processes. Therefore, by communicating with the subconscious part of the mind in ways that it prefers to receive them, you achieve more than by speaking to the conscious part of the mind.

To put it simply, here is the formula for "hypnosis":

Hypnosis = a trance state + language and concepts that the subconscious mind is receptive to

This also means that hypnosis is present in a lot of places you might not have realized before:

- Politicians use these persuasion principles and hypnotic language. When a politician has a very focused attention and they use the correct language and concepts that I talk about in this book we are being hypnotically persuaded. Indeed, many well-known politicians have consultants that train them to speak in more effective hypnotic and persuasive ways.
- Television – people say they don't think they can be hypnotized yet they cry or laugh when watching a film. This is essentially words, pictures and sounds bringing about emotions and feelings. A powerful movie with powerful words can get us to change our viewpoints, alter our belief systems and more.

The point to understand is that training in hypnosis, sales, rapport and even effective presentation all have multiple elements in common. They all focus on achieving an outcome – the only difference is that the hypnotic principles work directly with the subconscious mind, whereas the others may do so indirectly, but they speak more to the conscious mind.

To illustrate the power of these concepts allow me to demonstrate the power of one hypnotic word that we hypnotists love to use: the word "Because".

In the book "Influence: The Psychology of Persuasion" by Robert Cialdini there is a study that he talks about performed by Ellen Langer at Harvard.

In the study Langer asked to push in line at the library to photocopy some papers – he used three different phrases on a number of people in order to record how they would react.

In the first instance the following phrase:

"Excuse me, I have five pages. May I use the Xerox machine?"

In this case 60% of the time people let him through.

In the second instance, he said:

"Excuse me, I have 5 pages. May I use the Xerox machine, because I'm in a rush?"

In this case, in which he gave a reason to validate his request, 94% of the time people let him through!

However, even more surprising is the last case, in which he said the following:

"Excuse me, I have 5 pages. May I use the Xerox machine, because I have to make copies?"

Notice that there is not even a valid reason to allow him to push in line! Nevertheless, this phrase still achieved a 93% success rate.

That example works because according to hypnosis theory, the subconscious mind loves things to be validated or justified, as it allows those things to make sense and brings order.

That was just an example of one single word!

While this book does not necessarily focus on language, it is dedicated to helping you learn the key concepts which persuade us all at a conscious and subconscious level, allowing you to say the right things based on any given situation. After both learning hypnosis and undergoing a lot of sales training, I have realized that sales training actually already uses a number of hypnotic concepts (the same as with advertising). They are just different ways to describe the same principles. However, having a deep understanding of both has allowed me to uncover a few more hidden truths from each of them.

Understanding these principles and applying them in everyday life will allow you to highlight natural ways to persuade people at a subconscious level, and while it isn't a rigid science that works in every single instance, it does allow you to be more effective in conversations overall.

And what about getting someone into a "trance state" you may ask? Remember that I described this as a "focused state of attention". A light trance is extremely simple to create: just look people in the eyes when you talk to them! This is often enough to get a person's attention, and stop them thinking about their laundry, allowing you to "hypnotically persuade" people easily and effortlessly.

Want to learn some hypnotic language?

Get the FREE guide – 11 Hypnotic Power words of Persuasion: Discover hot words used by hypnotists that you can start using in the next 47 minutes to make your everyday communication more persuasive

http://www.muneer.com/powerwords/

What are the Principles of persuasion- and how can they be used?

The principles of persuasion serve as the reasons people do anything – these principles are brought about through many forms of language, text, advertising, images, suggestions and all kinds of media.

To illustrate what I mean, let's take the familiar concept of comedy/humor, and the ability to make people laugh. We all like to make people laugh – it builds your social status and makes people warm to you. Comedians get paid large sums of money to do just that. There are those who have the innate ability to do this, though to most of us it doesn't come naturally.

It is, however, something that you can learn.

- Comedy can sometimes have delivery methods that are dedicated to the medium, with tried and tested formulas of timing, themes, tone, satire, slapstick, etc. For example:
  - Stand up comedy
  - Television comedy
  - Movies (e.g. Anchorman)
  - Comedy literature (e.g. books by the genius Terry Pratchett)

- It also comes in many forms that are not necessarily dedicated to comedy, but are entertaining nonetheless:
  - Topical TV shows that happen to be funny, e.g. Top Gear (or Grand Tour) for example – a car show that is extremely funny.
  - Movies – Kung Fu Panda is an animated adventure that is also funny... at least my daughter thinks so (Ok, ok... I do too!).
  - There are also (*ahem) books on highly interesting educational topics. For example, just hypothetically speaking, you may find (*cough, ahem...) a really amazing

book on persuasion and influence that could be extremely hilarious because it had a really awesome writer (*ahem). Just hypothetically speaking, of course...

The point is that just as comedy/humor is a concept that can be applied in numerous ways, so the principles of persuasion are concepts that can also applied in multiple forms.

Principles of persuasion can be used individually:

- As a sales pitch to get a person to take action;
- As part of a stage presentation or group sales pitch;
- To create an advertising campaign for television;
- To create a sales article or sales letter.

The principles of persuasion are heavily used in advertising (as you will see from many of the examples in this book) and advertising takes many forms: Print, radio, television, YouTube, Google search, social media ads, etc.

The principles of persuasion can also be used as part of something else, for example:

- In a movie or documentary – *Super Size Me* was a famous documentary that uses 'Fear of Loss', one of the principles of persuasion, to influence you to change your eating habits;
- A motivational talk can use many of the principles throughout its stories to move a person towards making a change in their lives;
- A book, a leaflet or brochure can all have a different purpose but contain similar elements of persuasion;
- A website review of a product can persuade someone to buy said product.

Another way that the two concepts are similar is that they can be broken up into different techniques that create the same outcome. For example, in order to make a person laugh, you could use one of the following:

- Physical & active (slapstick) comedy
- Anecdotes
- Visual comedy
- Funny sounds
- Voices and impersonations
- Jokes or one-liners
- Reactions to situations or events

Each on their own could produce the outcome of getting a person to laugh, and combining different ones can be very powerful. In fact, one technique done extremely well can have a better outcome than doing many badly.

In the same respect, there are 6 principles of persuasion – FILVOR.

Each done on its own can have the intended outcome of persuading a person to take action. If you use multiple principles together and you do each of them well, this can be very, very powerful. However, as with comedy, sometimes it is better to do one very well that all of them poorly.

And so, by roundabout means, we come to the **6 Principles of Persuasion** that form the foundations of everything contained in this book:

F – Fear of Loss

I – Indifference

L – Likeability

V – Value

O – Other People's Perceptions

R - Reciprocity

Over the coming chapters I will go through each in detail and show you how you can apply them to all the different areas of your life.

Is it possible to persuade EVERYONE to do what you want?

"The top salesperson in the organization probably missed more sales than 90% of the sales people on the team, but they also made more calls than the others." - Zig Ziglar

The blunt answer to the above questions is…. **No.** (Shock, horror, disgust! How can I say that in a persuasion book?)

Ok people, before you lose your bananas – First of all… why on earth would you need to persuade *everyone*?

People who are unwilling to do something that makes absolutely no sense to them should be perfectly free to say no! For example, if you were unable to persuade a 12 year-old girl to buy a beard trimmer for herself, well I wouldn't say you're a failure!

A person struggling to pay rent on a studio apartment will likely turn down your offer to sell them a private jet, even if you were the world's greatest private jet salesperson. Your sales manager wouldn't doubt your abilities as a sales person in this instance, though he might doubt your sanity for trying…

There is also a flipside to this coin, and here is the good news: Even if you are really terrible at persuasion, there is always *someone* out there whom you are able to persuade, within reason. It's impossible to persuade everyone, but it's also improbable to persuade no one at all!

Whilst I was living in the UK, I knew a guy who was not the handsomest chap, nor was he the healthiest fellow I knew, or even the most charming person around, though he had more courage than anyone I knew. While most people I knew did not have the courage to ask a girl for her number, this guy would approach 20-30 women in a night, and *always* come back with a number. In one night he would do something that might take others months!

(*Disclaimer – Let me state before any of the morality police come at me: I am telling you my life experiences, and I knew a guy that did it – right or wrong, good or bad, I'm not commenting. All I am saying is, even when odds are stacked against you, people get results.)

(**Disclaimer #2 – No, it wasn't me... I AM the handsomest chap! My mum says so...)

An example of odds stacked against you in the digital world is those email scams that you see plaguing your Spam folder. Working in digital marketing, I mix with a number of industry peers and we share interesting stories. An industry friend called Manuel told me that during his travels to Africa, he once met a person behind those email scams that we all get in our junk mail and had a conversation with him (I really hate those guys btw).

For some crazy reason, the scam artist shared some information about what he did with Manuel (I guess he was probably drunk). Initially Manuel doubted the guy and said, "But there is no way those things actually work!"

To which the scam artist replied, "You would be surprised. You don't need it to work a lot. In fact maybe 1 out of 10,000 emails may work, but that's all it takes for us, and don't underestimate the power in numbers."

To see how terrible at persuasion these guys are, you need only check your junk mail! I just had a quick look and found one... First of all they call me "Honorable". Who does that in this day and age? I feel like I woke up in scene from *Pride and Prejudice*. And why are there so many generals with vast sums of money locked up in a country that they can't get to? So now their first logical move is to write to a complete stranger. Of course! That makes total sense. Let's continue...

He wants to give ME (as we have established, "a total stranger") money. A whole bunch of money, usually in the region of tens of millions of dollars... and for what? For sending my name, phone number, address, underwear size and credit card number.

However, SOME PEOPLE FALL FOR IT! Not many, but it does happen.

Now Manuel was travelling in a foreign country, and wanted to know more, so he didn't cause a fuss for the guy, which was why he was able to have that conversation. However, the point to all this is:

If the bad guys are able to persuade even *one* person with the most pathetic of attempts and no skills whatsoever (and they are *terrible* persuaders, I mean the worst in the world!), that means that us good guys can do FAR better. If you have great intentions, serious skills, attractive products and positive outcomes for others, you are GUARANTEED to get results.

What is important for us to understand is that results come as a law – The law of averages.

This law is important, because when it comes to getting results in persuasion:

> *"Efficiency is not the same as results." – Me.*

(Ok, yes, I just quoted myself, in a book that I am writing, so that is totally weird. However the concept is extremely important, so I want you to pay attention to it. Also, once I was accused of not being so smart, but only smart people get quoted in books, so I guess I showed THEM.)

For every area of persuasion there is a "law of averages", and this applies to selling, applying for jobs, getting votes, getting business cards or even getting a phone number. It is, basically, the percentage of a given number of people that will agree to something that you are suggesting.

Us geeky people in the digital marketing world call this a 'conversion rate', and it is scarily consistent! It does not really change a great deal from day to day, or segment to segment.

Let's say, for example, that one day you meet the guy that runs Amazon.com, and you ask him what his conversion rate is, and he says 5%. This means that every single day 5 out of every 100 people that visit the website buy something. It doesn't change a great deal from day to day UNLESS something on the website changes, for example they run a special offer, or launch a hot new product.

Provided things are consistent, the conversion rate remains consistent. It's not 15% one day and 2% the next – it always hovers around the same figure until something changes. The reason I was able to live on pure commission doing door-to-door sales is because I understood this law of averages. I knew that if I knocked on 100 doors, I would get ten sales if I had a conversion rate of 10%.

If everything stays the same (what you say, the type of person you say it to, your offer etc.), your conversion rate will remain the same. However when you learn how to be more persuasive, you are essentially learning to be more efficient. It's like changing your offer on a website to become more appealing. You suddenly have the ability to convert more people.

Reading this book will help you to become more efficient. The contents on these pages could improve your conversion rate from 10% to 30%, so instead of 1 out of every 10 people, you will convince 3 out of 10 people. The more skills you learn, the higher that number will be.

What I want to stress, and the reason for this whole chapter, is that any sales and persuasion training is about making you a much better sales person. However, beware of anything that claims to give you a 100% success rate. It simply doesn't exist!

The Persuasion Results Formula

To manage expectations efficiently, I have developed something called "The Persuasion Results Formula". This is a fancy chart that really helps you to identify where you are and what you need to improve in order to get results.

The reason I feel it is important to emphasize this, is that while working in door-to-door sales in London, I met a young man called Tom who wanted to try out door-to-door sales, and so came for an initial trial day. I could instantly see that Tom was someone who I considered to have amazing potential, as he was already an amazingly good conversationalist.

However, after speaking to only seven people he believed that he was unpersuasive, and a bad salesperson. This was all down to expectations. This guy may have been the smoothest talker, but he had tried selling to just seven people, hadn't made a sale, and made a judgment on his abilities based on this limited experience.

I could see he had better people skills than me, and most people in the office, but his expectations were misplaced. Managing expectations correctly is important in getting results, because Tom would have been exceptional at sales if he hadn't set his mind up to fail, which led to him giving up prematurely. This also taught me a valuable lesson: A great salesperson isn't someone who thinks they can sell to everyone they meet. The best salesperson is the one who sells the most – period!

These are not necessarily the same thing.

In fact, I have trained a number of salespeople with almost no knowledge of sales to be the best sales people in the country in a very short space of time using "The Persuasion Results Formula", and I would like to tell you about one guy in particular.

The Persuasion Results formula is explained through a very intelligent and official looking diagram and table, which means I would rather explain it you via a story. I have to keep you entertained after all, and while diagrams are educational, I don't recall anyone's idea of a great night out involving a diagram. Good nights out do, on the other hand, involve stories, so allow me to explain this highly complex and sophisticated formula to you by telling you about Kevin.

When I worked in door-to-door sales, I would work on building a team of sales representatives. This involved the recruitment and training of these people in order to show them how to sell and what was involved. One day a recruit by the name of Kevin joined my team. Kevin was an enthusiastic young man who was keen and willing to learn everything I could show him.

The first day for any new trainee is when they shadow you, watching you sell to people, and demonstrating how to do the job successfully. I would always explain the two main foundations of the persuasion results formula to any new trainee. These foundations are the things that you can control and will affect the number of people you are able to influence successfully. These two things are:

1. The skills that you acquire to convert people
2. The number of relevant people that you speak to

I explained that while skills were something he would pick up over time – he had complete control over the number of people he spoke to in the short term.

On Kevin's first day, I taught him what to say (plus I showed him the very basics of the 6 Principles of Persuasion that we will be covering in this book), and we practiced his pitch a few times before I allowed him to pitch to about five people by the day's end. On this particular day he made no sales, but the point of the exercise was to get him to practice what he should say after seeing me do it a number of times.

Now before I continue, let me show you the basics of the formula:

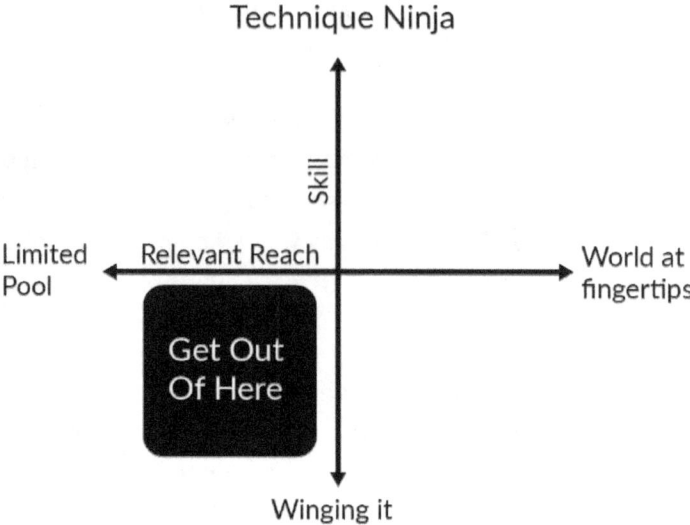

As you can see from the diagram above, there are two main foundations of the persuasion results formula (what the axes represent), which are relevant reach and skill. Let us first look at the vertical axis (the up-and-down line, for my directionally-dyslexic friends):

-When a person has no skills and tries to persuade someone, he is "winging it", *aka* trying his luck (the bottom of the diagram).

-When a person has all the skills in the world, then he is a "technique ninja" *aka* 'Me' (this is where you've learned things like the persuasion principles, language patterns, yes sets, and so on).

Now lets look at the horizontal axis (the one that's not the up-and-down line):

This axis represents *RELEVANT* reach. The world "relevant" here is very important because I feel that people should never judge their persuasion skills when they are not talking to someone that is relevant.

Now to the left of this arrow is when you don't have many people to persuade – for example if you only have one person to persuade, this would mean you have a limited pool. An example of this would be if you were trying to persuade your spouse. Then you would have only one person to persuade.

Finally to the right of the diagram, if you have endless numbers of people that you can speak to, then the world is at your fingertips. More often than not getting to this point is just a case of having the confidence to speak to as many people as possible.

Getting results in persuasion, sales, tele-sales or networking is never going to happen if you don't have any skills or you don't speak to anyone. This is why I call the bottom left part of the diagram "Get out of here", because if you are aiming to get results, you have to be anywhere other than there!

On his first day Kevin was in this position – he had very low skills (it was his first day) and he had only spoken to 5 people, 2 of whom were not relevant (a limited pool). Over the next two days I continued to work with Kevin, making sure he knew what to say and understood the basics of the selling game after which I let Kevin loose. In his first week, Kevin went on to become the top salesperson out of thousands of people in the country. This made me proud but it also surprised a bunch of people. How did this relative newbie overtake some of the best salespeople in the country in only his first week?

I won't lie to you; I was surprised myself. The guy overtook me in the shortest space of time. This was great as a team leader, though I was still curious to know how he did this. Fortunately I believe very strongly that humility can lead to profitability. What this means is, if you can learn from anyone whom you believe is better than you, no matter who they are, you should take that opportunity – even if they are more junior than you, and in my case, was someone that was my trainee only one week prior.

So I went to Kevin and said, "Kevin, you are doing an absolutely amazing job and I am super happy for you – please teach me and tell me how are you doing it?"

Kevin looked at me and laughed, "Muneer, you taught this to me: You said that the one thing I had in my control was the number of people I speak to, so I found out how many people you and the other top sales reps were speaking to and I doubled it. You guys were speaking to 70 a day, so I decided to do what was within my control and speak to 140 people a day!"

Just like that I had been taught a lesson that I had just been teaching to someone a week ago.

Here's the thing - Kevin was fast! This guy would run between houses like he was being chased by a mob with machetes. While all the top salespeople spoke to about 70 people and got 7 sales, Kevin spoke to 140 and got 9. We were considered more efficient, however Kevin was the better sales representative. He was considered the better persuader.

To go back to my quote: Efficiency is not the same as results.

As Kevin progressed over the next few weeks and he learned more skills his conversion rate improved too. When any person learns and takes action their results improve dramatically.

We are all constantly learning. Along with a couple of the other top sales reps in the office we decided to take this lesson that I had learned from Kevin, to whom I had in fact taught the same lesson one week prior (yes I know, as confusing as *Inception*...) and apply it.

We had large teams and we were expected to set the pace, plus we were always competing for the top spot. So we started to run between houses too and got up to seeing about 110 people a day (I won't even pretend that we could be as fast as Kevin – that kid was faster than my wife running towards a shoe sale!). By getting up to 110 people, we started doing around 11 sales a day, up from 7, which placed my team back at the top spot in the country.

This brings me back to the rest of "The Persuasion Results Formula":

As mentioned previously, on Kevin's first day, he was in the bottom left box – "Get out of here". However, after his first week, he started running and speaking to more people than anybody and so he moved to the extreme right. Here he was getting results AND "Learning Fast". I think the name is self- descriptive.

However it is important to note that in this area, you can be at the same level as someone with years of experience, because here you are mitigating any lack of efficiency, or a low conversion rate, with an abundance of volume.

Now allow me to explain the top left corner – this is when you have a whole bunch of skills but you have a limited pool to work with. I consider myself pretty good at the game of persuasion, however I am unable to persuade my wife to watch *Die Hard* with me (Believe me I have tried... and I keep trying... maybe that is why I am studying this field so much!).

When you only have one person that you are trying to persuade – then magic can be inconsistent. You must rely on skill as much as possible, but results aren't guaranteed. This is why I call that section "Unreliable Magic". Magic definitely happens there, though not as consistently.

Back to the Chronicles of Kevin: Before the top sales reps and I had learned our lesson from Kevin, we were speaking with 70 people a day. If you look at the diagram, this was hardly "the left side" of the diagram; it was definitely on the right in the box called "consistent magic" – we were consistently getting daily results – however in comparison to Kevin, who was much further to the right because he was seeing more people, it seemed like we were in the top left.

When we decided to push harder and move faster, in the diagram we moved all the way to the right and that allowed us to take the top spot in the country in the following weeks. I explain this model to you for the same reason I am taking the time out to write this book. I want you to get results.

Here is the reality: I can give you some of the most awesome techniques in the world (and some of them are truly awesome!), but if you don't try them out, then they won't work. These techniques will make you much more efficient, but efficiency only works in combination with effort, so go out have a few conversations using the techniques in this book, and watch your conversion rate skyrocket.

Want to improve your conversational skills?

Get my FREE guide – 11 Hypnotic Power words of Persuasion: Discover hot words used by hypnotists that you can start using in the next 47 minutes to make your everyday communication more persuasive

http://www.muneer.com/powerwords/

FEAR OF LOSS

"One of the key elements of human behavior is, humans have a greater fear of loss than enjoyment of success. All the academic studies will show you that the fear of loss of capital is far greater than the enjoyment of gains."
Laurence D. Fink

Growing up in the Sultanate of Oman, where we had a grand choice of two TV channels in my younger days, my mother would be hard-pressed for entertainment, and so she used to like to go shopping at the markets quite often – also referred to as the *souq*!

As a 9 year old boy, there were a whole number of things that I would prefer to get up to other than shopping at the *souq* – video games, football or listening to fingernails dragged down a chalkboard, to name a few. Despite this, I was frequently dragged along and I suppose that was good, because it did teach me the first Principle of Persuasion, "Fear of Loss", at a tender age.

You see, my mother used to love haggling, and upon arriving at the *souq* we would enter the first shop and, after some casual browsing, she would enquire about the price of an item. The shopkeepers would, in turn, provide her with a price higher than one might expect, to which my mother would react with a performance of utter shock and indignation worthy of an Oscar.

"What! I was just at the shop down there, and they had it for half the price!"

There was no "shop down there", and no "half price" existed – this was the first place we'd walked into! I also learned VERY early on in our excursions that I should never actually point out that fact during my mother's negotiations...

Now the art of *souq* haggling is a highly intriguing and subtle art of back-and-forth that can often be quite enjoyable to both seller and buyer. It's a definite art, because they must often hear similar stories, which means that you have to be as convincing as possible to instill a "fear of losing the sale" in them, despite the fact that they have heard the story a thousand times before.

It is similar to seeing the phrase "This price is only available for 24 hours" all the time on shopping websites. Though it often isn't true, or the price isn't really any lower than usual, it still encourages you to take action when there is a well structured countdown, just in case!

So after proclaiming the fact that she had been offered a lower price elsewhere, my mother would start to walk out of the store. This would ignite in the shopkeepers a "Fear of Loss" – a worry that they may lose out on the sale, prompting them to then try re-engage my mother somehow by lowering the price slightly.

Not wanting to lower their prices too much while still maintaining the sale, they would suddenly confess their ability to reduce the price, and go on to laud the many benefits their product has over those of the other shops (justifying price difference) and would finish by saying something like: "We actually only have these two pieces left and one has just been reserved by someone that is coming to buy it soon and he was going to check if his family also wanted one… "

BOOM! Just like that, the "fear of loss" technique had been bounced back on us and now the ball is back in our court. This scenario would go back and forth for quite some time. Often I would suspect that my mother bought items purely as a payment for the experience of a good haggle rather than for the actual item itself. I also believe that many shopkeepers also enjoy it to an extent – as long as they make a profit, which they invariably do.

I am often quite grateful that I grew up in Oman in an environment where this kind of bargaining was the norm. Can you imagine me doing that at a supermarket in the UK? Can you imagine if I walked into Tesco, picked up a tub of *hummus* and asked some poor teenager working his way through college about the price?

He would look at the shelf and tell me the price, and then with a little smile on my face, I'd say: "My friend! You know at Sainsbury's I could get this for half the price! Come on... give me best price." Then I would have to look at the pained look on his face when he starts to think, "I really have to study hard so I can leave this job and not deal with these crazy foreigners!"

"The fear of loss is greater than the desire for gain" – Zig Ziglar

As human beings, everything that we do is linked to either gaining pleasure or avoiding discomfort. More often than not, the avoidance of discomfort is the biggest driver that people have, and the Fear of Loss principle capitalizes on that.

As you can see in this example, there are multiple forms that Fear of Loss can take. It can take shape in the form of scarcity, it can take place in the form of fear of losing out, and then there is also the sense of urgency.

Scarcity – A limited number of the item exists, after which a person will lose out.

Sense of Urgency – A limited time frame exists, after which a person will lose out.

Importance of Action – An action must take place, otherwise a person will lose out.

The phenomenon in a social context has been realized to such an extent that it has become a hashtag phenomenon: #FOMO. In case you're not familiar with the expression, it is an acronym for "Fear of missing out", a pop culture term that describes the feeling that pushes people to take action so that they do not miss out on an experience or feel left out. FOMO typically refers to the fear of missing out when people have fun, as you are not there, and then learning all about it on social media. The days of blissful ignorance are over!

"We are hard wired to want those things we are at risk of not being able to have." – Me.

Let's forget my random stories of a little boy shopping with his mother, and look at some serious science-type people in white coats that conducted big experiments using cookies and lots of science stuff to prove these facts.

In 1975 an experiment was conducted by social psychologist Stephen Worchel at the University of North Carolina. He conducted the experiment with around 200 students, who were asked to rate the taste of cookies.

50% of participants in the study were given a full jar of 10 cookies to start with, and the other 50% were given an empty-looking jar with only 2 cookies. They were then asked to rate the taste of the cookies. Those people that had a jar with only two cookies rated those cookies as tasting better! What was even more interesting, however, is that a portion of the 200 students were tested in cases where they were given a full jar which was then swapped out in front of the person at the last minute.

So picture this: There is Mary who is given a full-looking jar of 10 cookies thinking to herself "Wow, I got all these awesome cookies", and then the door bursts open and Mr Lab Coat (that isn't his real name... I don't think) comes in and says: "The demand for these cookies has been quite high, so I'm going to need to take some cookies from you!"

So he swaps out Mary's 10 cookies and leaves her with 2 cookies. For some reason Mary and everyone in the same situation as her gave the cookies the highest taste rating of all the subject groups! Her brain was chemically wired to wanting that thing that had become scarce right before her very eyes. Scarcity (a variant of Fear of Loss) makes us like things more.

Despite all of this scientific evidence, I still doubt I'd be successful in trying to persuade my aunt that I would like her food more if she gave me less of it...

"But Auntie, in 1975 Dr Steven Wor...."

"MUNEER! You really need to stop reading all your nonsense... Look at you! You're withering away... here have some more of this stew..."

Another common example in which you see "Fear of Loss" present in everyday lives is that all-too-familiar tale of 'boy likes girl, girl pays him no attention, boy moves on another girl, first girl now wants boy' (Or, so I am told from books on the subject...) Sadly, this is human nature – we don't appreciate what we already have, and want what we think we may not be able to have. Attraction, as you will learn later, is a form of influence and persuasion just as sales are, and therefore many of the principles of persuasion also apply in those cases.

Digital persuasion

The digital world has allowed us to put in place and test the principles of persuasion in ways that were unavailable before, with numbers instantly available for us to see the uptick based on these theories. There are cases in which websites have experienced a 200% increase in sales when they have created a sense of urgency by adding a countdown clock.

Websites like *booking.com* and a number of other online shopping portals have experimented with adding the scarcity factor by mentioning how many items are left before they sell out. For example, have you ever seen the small label on a hotel room saying, "Only 1 room available – hurry and book!" Or, you might have seen the same on the cheapest seats on an airline's booking page: "Only 2 seats available!"

It's important to note that Fear of Loss is not just a driver of sales but also a negotiation tool (just like the *souq* examples earlier). And it's not just for small and cheap things; it works on large purchases too.

When I had decided that I would like to buy my third property in the UAE, I knew what I wanted – a four bedroom villa in a specific community that had a large garden. Since all the interior floor plans of the four bedroom villas in that community were exactly the same, the only difference between them was the location and garden size. I had decided that my aim was to buy the largest plot for the cheapest price.

So, I called up every real estate agent and told them what I was looking for, and every agent came back to me saying: "That's not how it works. The bigger the plot, the more you pay!"

To which I would reply, "I understand how it works, but I am a serious buyer and I have contacted multiple agents. I will be going with the first person who can negotiate the biggest plot for the lowest price for me."

Sure enough, within 3 weeks of pitting agents against each other, their fear of losing out on my business as a serious buyer made them negotiate a great price for me, so I ended up getting the largest plot for the lowest price!

Fear of Loss can actually lead people to do crazy things too though. Allow me to tell you the story of what *Time* magazine described as: "The WORST marketing disaster EVER!"

On the 23rd April, 1985 Coca Cola pulled its old formula of their hugely popular drink from the shelves and replaced it with a new version. They had carried out extensive taste testing on the new formula, and were convinced it would be a success. Of course, the public revolted *en masse*, rejecting the new drink completely. There was one gentleman by the name of Gay Mullins who even started a whole movement: "Old Cola Drinkers of America".

The guy filed a class-action lawsuit against Coca Cola, and was so passionate about the whole thing that he made buttons, t-shirts, created a hotline and a whole lot more.

Now get this – Gay Mullins had taken the blind test TWICE, and had been unable to distinguish the new coke from the old original coke! However, he had already made a public commitment and didn't want to back down (more on that later in the section about other people's perceptions).

Now you may be wondering how all this could happen. After all, Coca Cola had conducted lots of research, and they had the results of many taste tests that proved people preferred the new Coke, so how did they have this nationwide uproar driven by people that went crazy!

Well, let's look back to the cookie example – remember when there were only two cookies? People thought that they tasted better. Scarcity makes us want things more – so as Coca Cola found out when they pulled everyone's favorite drink off the shelves, people are hard wired to want the thing that they were likely unable to have more of.

You may also remember that the group that rated the cookie taste the highest was the group of people that had an abundance of cookies and then all of a sudden, it was taken away and the cookies were scarce. This is what happened with the old Coke; it was everywhere and then all of a sudden it was taken away and it became extremely scarce, prompting people to want that thing that they can't have.

While Time magazine initially called this "The worst marketing disaster ever", it actually may have inadvertently been the most ingenious marketing ploy ever. Up until that point the rivalry between Pepsi and Coca Cola had been huge. However, when Coca Cola reintroduced the old formula under the moniker Classic Coke, their shares surged, and the dominance swung firmly in Coca Cola's way.

Let's return to the digital fear of loss:

Some of the greatest online product launches that have made millions of dollars in 24 hours have used these principles too. For example, the products of Frank Kern, John Reese and Jeff Walker, to name but a few of these extremely successful major internet marketing personalities, have all made massive profits in very short time frames.

They do this by training audiences to believe that the fear of loss is real. They hold major product launches that have a big build-up which leads to a specific launch date. On that date they offer their product for sale for only 5 days, after which they close their page down and you are unable to buy, even if you want to and stock is available.

This encourages people to buy straight away, while also training people who do not buy that the fear of loss is real and that the next time a product is on offer, they need to buy it straight away or they will miss out!

The sense of urgency also allows them to generate a large amount of money in a short space of time, which allows them to sell their success story the next time round. You will see me refer to these launches occasionally in some of the chapters ahead because they rely heavily on the principles of persuasion that we talk about in this book.

In Conclusion

Fear of loss refers to the fear people have of losing out. This can be in the following forms:

- Scarcity – limitation on quantity, after which a person will miss out.
- Sense of Urgency – Time limit, after which a person will miss out.
- Importance of Action – Action must take place, or a person will miss out.

It is this fear of missing out that causes people to take action.

Fear of loss can be manifested in many different places:

- In sales
- In negotiations
- To increase how much somebody likes something
- In advertising
- In attraction
- In a digital booking engine
- To launch a product

I have provided many examples conducted by various scientists over the years, as well as my mother's haggling, though I feel ethically responsible to put in this disclaimer: It is vital to note that, whatever happens, those studies cannot be used to convince my aunt not to stuff your face with food.

Get my FREE guide – 11 Hypnotic Power words of Persuasion: Discover hot words used by hypnotists that you can start using in the next 47 minutes to make your everyday communication more persuasive

http://www.muneer.com/powerwords/

INDIFFERENCE

"Desperation is like stealing from the Mafia: you stand a good chance of attracting the wrong attention." -Douglas Horton

LOSE THE IMAGE OF DESPERATION OR BE FACED WITH IMPEDING FRUSTRATION

When I was growing up, we always used to have cats in our house. Not just one, but often a number of them. It is my frequent interaction with cats that makes me feel like I am somewhat of a cat whisperer. While this is perhaps the most hopeless of all the superpowers that a person could ask for, it has provided me with a little bit of an understanding into animal (humans being some of them) nature and influence.

Unfortunately this amazing superpower does not fare well at parties because people aren't really interested in a cat whisperer, and since the cats are afraid of everyone else I wouldn't be able to get a cat to come to me at a party anyhow. This also means that I don't exactly have much of an audience when I get strange cats to come and be my friend on the street.

My ability isn't actually to get cats to do much else other than to trust me, like me and come to me. Especially cats I have just met. I have not acquired this superpower because some radioactive wonky-eyed cat in an alleyway jumped out and bit me. I just learned it through patience, a fondness of cats and understanding the 'Indifference' rule. You see, if a cat on the street sees a stranger, it's curious, yet wary, so it's torn between running away and investigating this curious stranger at the same time. After all, you might have food!

So if you approach the cat too quickly, it takes this as a threat and runs away. It senses that you are not indifferent, and scrams. However, if you indulge its curiosity by being curious yourself you'll get a different result: Instead of walking towards the cat, you start stepping backwards, crouching down while you engage in cat eye contact (pro tip: try not to use seductive eye contact – it doesn't affect the process, and your neighbors will think you're weird).

This process of engaging the cat in eye contact while stepping backwards and kneeling down will pique the interest of the cat and get it to come towards you! Now while I say that this is a superpower (albeit a pretty lame one), in actual fact it is something that anyone can learn to do (if you don't have anything better to do with your time).

The thing is, this phenomenon is present in us as humans too. Watch any guy that appears too keen on a nightclub dance floor and you'll see what I mean! The ladies in question will sense that he's not indifferent and run off (Ahem... this also happened to a friend of mine, Bob!). There is definitely something to be said for playing hard to get.

I've heard many examples of people going to a store and being scared off by an over enthusiastic salesman, despite an initial interest in a product. If they're so desperate to make a sale, there must be something wrong with it!

I am guilty of doing this myself – in my very early days as a door-to-door salesman, I would sometimes get desperate for a sale. After all, we worked on pure commission and if I hadn't sold anything in the first part of the day, desperation would start to show in my approach, as I would be trying to get people to buy it for my sake instead of because of the benefits of my product.

Needless to say my earlier days were full of learnings, and when I was finally able to control my indifference, my sales skyrocketed, I became more consistent and shot to the top of the UK rankings of all sales reps in the country. The reason we get turned off by a lack of indifference is because trust needs to be in place in order for us to take action, and when someone is being pushy or desperate we do not want to buy from them because we feel that they have a vested interest and so whatever they are saying cannot be true as it is biased.

Indifference in this instance is the art of showing interest in a person doing something, without them feeling like you have a major gain from it. So how, then, can you create interest and persuade people – while being indifferent?

Well in some cases it is often as simple as stating your indifference. In a sales example a person could actually say, "You are free to get this or not, either way I have nothing to gain – I just want to make sure that the right people who are looking for [exceptional quality/bigger savings etc.] hear about this."

Now compare that last phrase to: "Please buy this, you have to buy it please…" (For some reason I imagine this phrase in a whiny voice… possibly because I have a friend Bob who was desperate very early on in his career as a door-to-door salesman!)

The first phrase, although fairly simple (I do not use any of the language patterns that I teach in my other programs), delivers a greater air of confidence than the one that follows it (the whiny voice one). It has a greater element of trust between the two of them. Another method to build trust by displaying indifference is to discuss a flaw that you have before selling or trying to persuade someone.

Studies conducted have shown that the level of trust goes up when someone openly admits their flaws, and using this principle big advertising firms have built huge campaigns utilizing this concept. For example, in 1962 Avis (the rent-a-car company) was significantly trailing behind the market leader Hertz, and in an effort to bridge the gap, their advertising agency came up with a slogan that utilized this principle and embraced their flaw.

"When you're only No.2, you try harder"

The slogan became an instant hit, and within a year the market share gap between the two rival companies had gone down significantly: Hertz initially had a 61% market share (versus Avis' 29%) and this went down to

49% market share, whilst Avis climbed to 36% – a huge turnaround in growth and profits. Avis went from a company losing money to a highly profitable organization, all by using this principle!

Another major brand that has used this principle was L'Oréal. You may even be familiar with their tagline "Because you're worth it". What you may not realize is how this tagline evolved. L'Oréal was aware of the major objection that people had to their product, which was that it was more expensive than their competitors.

L'Oréal was well aware of the women's movements that had started to form in the early 70's and so they decided to devise a campaign to capitalize on the fact that women were becoming more prominent and independent in society. Therefore, their advertising agency embraced their flaw of being the most expensive and launched advertising campaigns where spokeswomen would come on screen and talk about using expensive products on themselves and being happy about it, because they were worth it!

The 'Expensive-but-worth-it' campaign hit a chord with women and the brand took off. Over time the slogan changed slightly to be "Because you're worth it", though the origin of the slogan was built on this pillar of indifference.

Indifference can some times be actively turning off the irrelevant people in order to turn on the relevant people. Modern-day online sales letters and successful product launches overtly turn away "irrelevant people" to turn on the relevant ones. Frank Kern, one of the digital marketing world's most successful copywriters, often uses phrases such as, "This product is not for you if you want things handed to you on a platter."

Many of the most successful online product launches that have made millions of dollars in only a few days have used that form of phrasing, where they speak about who the product is *not* for! Dr. Robert Cialdini, the author of *Influence,* gives an example of building trust in his books where he talks about tactics used by waiters in high-end restaurants of

Western countries to bolster tips. In many countries, it is customary to tip a certain percentage of your overall bill to the waiter serving you. Therefore it is actually logical that a waiter would want you to order more expensive things from the menu.

Dr. Cialdini talks about some of the more successful waiters that he has studied, where they would give restaurant goers the menu, wait for the order, and if you have ordered the fish, for example, they would turn and look over their shoulder in a secretive manner before leaning in to say to you, "Sir/Ma'am, the fish is not as fresh as it usually is today. Might I suggest the pasta instead?"

They would then proceed to pick a dish that is slightly less expensive on the menu. Upon hearing this, restaurant goers would often feel like they are able to trust the waiter more because he has their best interests at heart. After all, he had just selected a dish that would potentially minimize his tip! Here is the kicker: Upon building this trust by showing indifference, many waiters would then say the following, "May I recommend a (rather expensive) wine for you this evening that will compliment your meal perfectly?" (Sneaky little so and so!)

Just like that, because of the trust he has established, they take his recommendation of a wine which is more expensive than they would otherwise have chosen, and our waiter more than makes up for any difference in tip that he would have lost from suggesting a less expensive meal.

Warren Buffet is said to be a great user of this tactic when it comes to influencing and persuading shareholders. He uses the tactic of indifference in all his letters to shareholders, especially when he is moving them towards taking action. This paragraph was taken from his 2012 letter to shareholders of Berkshire Hathaway:

"A number of good things happened at Berkshire last year, but let's first get the bad news out of the way..."

He would then recount some of the major challenges the company faced before moving onto other items, and ultimately moving them to make a decision. What happens by the end of the letter is that all his shareholders feel more trusting of him because, not only does he know his faults, he is open about them and willing to share them, indicating that he has no hidden agenda. This makes people very open to whatever he suggests next, and open to accepting his recommendations. I feel it's no coincidence that he is one of the most successful business people of our time.

Let us now look at some published studies in the field. In 2007 there was a study conducted by Paul Eastwick that was published in Psychological Science. In the study they had people speed dating (Dating, cookies... I'm beginning to think I should've been a scientist!). In the experiment they allowed potential couples to meet, and afterwards examined the reasons for rejection. What they found was that people are easily able to detect desperation in other people. They actually *proved* that the people who were the most desperate for a date were also the people who were the least likely to get one.

The ones that showed the most indifference, however, were the most likely to get a date. The opposite of indifference is desperation, and it is important to recognize the signs of desperation within ourselves before they occur. Signs of desperation in persuasion efforts often include:

- Begging - Indifference lies in being able to ask for a meeting, call, action without sounding like you are begging. As soon as you sound like you are begging, you will have lost.
- Impatience - You can't ask a potential partner to marry you before you get their name!
  Indifference is understanding that you must occasionally be patient. Pushing someone to do something before they are ready will work against you.
- Ultimatums - "I really need this sale or I won't make my rent!" – even if a phrase like that served to make you into a charity case (it almost never does) it would kill your prospects of having long-term business.

- The Quivering Voice - When we are nervous our voice tends to quiver (I have been there many times, believe me), and the only reason that we could be nervous in a persuasive conversation is if we have a lot to gain. When we have loads to gain and are nervous – we lose indifference.
- Taking the hint – Sometimes indifference is understanding that people don't want to do something. It is important to be able to read the hints that are being portrayed. When you do, you must decide if you should move on or address it with one of the objection busters. However, pretending that it doesn't exist oozes desperation.

Conclusion:

- Indifference is essentially the opposite of desperation.
- By turning away the wrong people you are able to turn on the right ones.
- Indifference is the ability to show an acceptable amount of interest while portraying that you have no major vested interest in them undertaking the action.
- We spoke about a scenario in where some people went on dates and called it a science experiment. These guys found that the more desperate you are, the least likely you are to get a date.
- Mentioning a flaw first builds trust and credibility – this technique has been used in advertising for years and L'Oréal and Avis have had their profits skyrocket through the application of this principle.
- I also spoke about my useless superpower that has something to do with the ability to get cats to come to me, and how indifference is a principle that is part of nature as well as that of other animals.

Get my FREE guide – 11 Hypnotic Power words of Persuasion: Discover hot words used by hypnotists that you can start using in the next 47 minutes to make your everyday communication more persuasive

http://www.muneer.com/powerwords/

LIKEABILITY

"In general, being likeable is more about being interested, rather than interesting. Indeed, a good way to convince someone that you are an awesome conversationalist is to simply shut up and let the other person talk." - Karen Salmansohn

I.e. Relate to a person's favorite subject: Themselves!

When I entered fatherhood, I imagined that my party days would be over. I was, however, very wrong. They still exist and are in full force, just in a slightly different format. I actually write this chapter having just returned from some hardcore partying. It was an intense event – there was music, people were falling all over the place and I even witnessed one of the partygoers throw up!

I tell you, these one year-old birthday parties are another level!

In this section I want to talk to you about meeting people, and the reason I bring this one year-old's birthday party up is because at this event I had to relate to new people from extremely different backgrounds. You see, I live in the UAE, which is one of the most diverse countries in the world. Approximately 85% of the population is expatriate, meaning that especially in its two biggest emirates Abu Dhabi and Dubai (where the vast majority of expatriates reside), the expats outnumber the locals by about nine to one.

This lends itself to having unique circles of friends, groups who hail from all over the world. For example, just in my close group of friends (these are people who travelled with me to Zanzibar for my wedding – so I mean close), there are people from Bahrain, Oman, South Africa, Poland, Australia, Egypt, Sweden, India, the US, Canada, the UK and Kenya, to name a few places.

What this mix of people in the UAE also means is that at events like this birthday party, there is always a melting pot of nationalities that you have to meet and relate to. I didn't personally know anyone at the party when I arrived, except for my daughter whom I have known all her life, and my wife who I have spoken to a few times here and there... I guess you could say I am close with those two. However everyone else was new and very international.

For example, the hosting couple were from New Zeland and England (which I assume would mean their daughter was New English?), and there were guests from South Africa, India, Germany, Bulgaria just to name a few. This of course is information that I learned about the big people at the party – I didn't converse too much with the small ones... well at least not at an intellectual level!

So conversations with new people in the UAE are quite interesting because they usually differ to other parts of the world as they always start with:

"How long have you been in the UAE?"

and

"Where are you from?"

In these two questions, I am able to particularly relate to large groups of international audiences quickly, and that is because, wherever they are from, I have either been there, or I know someone from there, or it is somewhere I would love to go to or, on the odd occasion I do not know where a country is, I genuinely want to know more about it!

In every single one of those cases I am relating to that person in some form or another. I am able to break the ice because I am taking interest in the person at a much deeper level by finding out about them. The same is true when I ask about how long a person has been in the UAE, if they are new, then I ask them what they would like to see, and find out what experiences they have had so far. If they have been in the UAE for a very long time, I may ask how they have seen the city develop over time. If they have been around about as long as I have (more medium term) then I can relate to them on that similar level.

Likeability is the process where a person relates to people that are either like them in some shape or form, or is interested in the things that he or she likes. Basically, it's a person saying, "I like that guy/gal coz he is like me" OR "I like that guy/gal coz he likes what I like!" This is ultimately a principle of persuasion, because people are much more easily persuaded by people they like, and you face an uphill battle trying to persuade someone who does not like you.

Let us imagine a scenario that could potentially happen in the UAE: If I were to meet someone new here and after a brief discussion where I learn a little bit about them, I say to them, "You know, it is crazy, but I actually have a friend that is also from [insert random country here], they also grew up in the same city as you and obviously speak [insert the person's language here], I believe they even went to the same university as you and they are now living in the UAE – would you like me to introduce you?" The likeliest answer would be "YES", because people want to meet people with something in common.

A strange thing happened to me the other day, and I couldn't make this up if I tried as it was such a surreal moment! I had just finished my "Client Creation Formula" seminar, which I ran in Dubai at the Knowledge Village. I was at my car packing away all the things I had used in my seminar, like 'the mountain of motivation blocks' as well as the leftover copies of my book, *Multiple Streams of Inspiration*, when a guy drove by and shouted, "Muneer?"

"Yes" I replied, thinking it was one of the seminar attendees that wanted to say hi.

"Muneer Al Busaidi?"

I started wondering – I don't think I told many people my second name, and my communication and my social profiles just use my first name, Muneer, so I became very curious. The guy parked the car, got out and said, "Bro, it is so great to meet you. I'm also Muneer Al Busaidi! People have been getting us confused on social media for ages. I have been wanting to meet you for a while. After all, there aren't many of us around!"

Here's the crazy thing: I got excited that this guy had the same name as me. We proceeded to have a great conversation, exchanged numbers and are now friends, all simply because the guy had exactly the same name as me!

Derren Brown filmed an experiment on his show, *Pushed to the Edge*, where they got unsuspecting participants to commit the extreme act of pushing someone off of a roof by putting them through a combination of extreme situations that push people to their limits, and persuasion tactics. As such, towards the start of the show when the participant first comes on, they are introduced to a person who pretends to have the same surname as the participant. This was the first in a series of steps to getting pure compliance in an extreme act. However, its inclusion was important in establishing the initial likeability that led to some further acts.

So, before I explain how to create the "Likeability" factor, it's important to discuss why "liking" is so important. When someone "likes" you it becomes a form of friendship, and as Jeoffery Gitmore puts it in his book, *The Little Red Book of Selling*: "All things being equal, people want to do business with their friends. And all things being NOT so equal, people STILL want to do business with their friends."

Getting a person to take action only happens when people are either neutral towards you, like you or consider you an authority (more on authority in the section "Other People's Perceptions"). If a person does not like you and does not trust you, they will literally refuse to go through with something, even if they wanted to in the first place!

A good friend of mine was once looking to buy a smart watch. He conducted research online, read all the reviews and was extremely keen to buy it. He found some guy online that was selling the watch, and went to go meet the person. After a brief conversation, he just decided that he shouldn't buy it. I asked him why, after all that effort, he changed his mind. He told me, "I don't know, the guy just gave me a bad vibe and it put me off."

So how then are you able to get someone to "like" you? Well, ultimately there are two general directions: the conscious route and the unconscious route (the stealth game!).

Firstly the conscious route – Dr Cialdini, in his book *Influence*, lists five ways that we create "Likeability":

1. Similarity: At its most basic level, you want to find out what a person likes, is interested in or values and relate to that.
2. Physical attractiveness: This is why attractive women are employed as models to promote products. It is also why a well-dressed presenter will often command the attention of the audience more than a scruffily-dressed presenter.
3. Compliments: We all like people who like us, and most of us like to be around people that tell us great things about ourselves. Just be careful not to over do it! Remember the 'indifference'…
4. Contact and co-operation: We tend to like people with whom we are working alongside to fulfill a common goal.
5. Conditioning and association: What car does James Bond drive? A person who I would like to be more like.

I want to quickly touch back on the concept of similarity – I honestly believe that it is extremely important to show a genuine interest in a person's interests if you are trying to get them to like you. Faking it rarely works. Finding a way to get fascinated about a person's interests in my eyes is fairly simple. Here are the ways that I relate to a subject that someone speaks about:

1. I have done that thing they are fascinated with or experienced it in some way, e.g. "Oh you play beach volleyball, that's pretty awesome – I've have played a few times myself in Oman with friends. I'm not that great but I enjoyed it – how did you learn to

play?" (Offer a bit of information that relates to them and then give an open ended question)

2. I would be interested to try out that experience they are talking about, e.g. "Oh wow that's interesting, you build model trains, I don't know much about that but I would actually like to try that one day, I can imagine that it's a very focused activity – how did you get into it?" (If I honestly find it a bit interesting and wouldn't mind trying out what they do I would say this)

3. If however, I have one of those "What the hell" moments, I will get really fascinated about their fascination. "Wow you like to knit mittens for kittens? That is such a unique activity and I have never met anyone that does that, how did you get into something like that?"

4. If I don't even want to try and relate, then I'll swiftly move on to the next subject. "Oh ok so you like to read about 18th century methods of torture? What ELSE do you like to do on your weekend?" (Let's just quickly move past that minefield!)

I have also mentioned that there are subconscious techniques that allow people to decide that they like you as well (ooh, the hypnotist emerges!). At a subconscious level, the principle of liking can be described as the creation of rapport. Rapport is essentially the feeling of being in-sync with an individual – which is a fancy way of saying, getting someone to like you.

How is this a subconscious activity?

To explain this, allow me to talk you through how we breathe, which is another subconscious activity - our breathing changes constantly depending on the situations we are in. When we are stressed we breathe differently, just like when we are in pain, and so on. We can also consciously adjust the way we breathe so that we can feel different. For example, if you have been involved in the miracle of childbirth, or watched any movie on the subject, then you will know the importance of changing the way you breathe to help the situation!

Even if you are a guy, believe me – in that situation, where your wife is about to break your hand because she is squeezing it so hard, and saying "Babe that hurts!" might just result in you being decapitated, Mortal Kombat-style, then you'll soon find out that breathing can help you too...

The point is that breathing is a subconscious activity that you can take control of to help in certain situations. If you breathe like you breath when you are calm, even in a stressful situation it will allow you to feel calmer.

Now the process of rapport is something you already do – you may recall a time that you felt a close connection with someone soon after meeting them. If you think back on that moment, or even see yourself having a conversation, you actually may have noticed a few interesting things. For example, your body language was possibly similar, you were speaking at around the same pace, your breathing would have even been aligned.

Think of a conversation you have had where you and a friend were recalling a funny experience – a conversation where you were both speaking at a certain pace, and then you started talking about the amusing experience and you both get excited around the same time and the conversation for both of you speeds up, there is an excitement in both your voices and laughter from both sides.

This is something we have all done and experienced subconsciously. Learning and being conscious of our behavior in those moments is something that we want to recreate, and if we can apply it to other situations we begin to create powerful influence. Just like understanding how calming your breathing can change a stressful situation, understanding how we subconsciously communicate when we have experienced rapport before can allow us to create rapport in other situations too.

The subconscious creation of rapport is similar to the earlier concept where we say, 'we like people who are like us'. Here are the ways in which we are able to create subconscious rapport:

- Matching and mirroring body language
- Matching tone of voice
- Matching pace of speaking
- Matching a person's modalities
- Eye contact

Ok, a bunch of words there that I need to explain, but before I get into that I want to paint a picture which I am going to be referring to:

To start with, imagine I took you to observe two couples having dinner, and I asked you to tell me which couple you believe has a better connection.

Couple A – This couple are both leaning in at the table, and looking into each other's eyes. They are both speaking softly to each other, and their body posture is aligned and looks like a mirror image of the other person.

Couple B – This couple look like complete opposites. One is leaning in while the other leans back. One is speaking loud and fast, the other soft and slow. One is looking at their food while the other looks around the room.

If I asked you to guess which one of those was the couple that had rapport and are in-sync, I am sure that you could tell me. (It's couple A by the way… and if you didn't get it, then you are seriously going to need my instant connection course!)

So let's go into each of the phrases that I brought up earlier:

Matching and mirroring body language
When people are in rapport, their body language starts to align and they begin to look like they are the mirror image of each other. It's a crazy phenomenon, but next time you are out for dinner, look around and notice that the people that are deeply engrossed with each other's

company are mirror images of each other. Remember, we like people who are like us. When we realize how our brain causes us to behave and move when people like each other, it allows us to take control of the process at a conscious level and do this deliberately to create the feeling of liking. (**Warning**: Use this carefully, because if it is too obvious then you can upset someone if they feel like you are mimicking them!)

Matching tone of voice & matching pace of speaking

I am combining the explanations of the two because they are both related to how you speak. Similar to body language, tone and pace of voice is another level of subconscious matching when we like a person. Refer to couple A, who are speaking softly and slowly towards each other vs. couple B, who are speaking at completely different speeds and volumes. Now while body language is a more powerful rapport builder, we don't always have the luxury of speaking to people when they are physically in front of us. Therefore, it is important to learn how to build rapport using other technologies such as over the phone.

To illustrate this, I have had to perform cold calling a number of times in my life, and occasionally I would call someone that would answer in a very hurried voice, "Hello, yes, who is this?" In a scenario like this I would answer in return in a very hurried voice, "Hi, yes, this Muneer, I understand you are busy so I am going to make this quick!"

Matching tonality is key in this scenario – if I spoke slow or stumbled, a call like that would have ended before I finished the sentence.

Matching a person's modalities

First allow me to explain what a modality is: We all have different senses with which we perceive the world. Seeing, hearing and touching are the primary representations for our everyday use, also referred to as Visual, Auditory and Kinesthetic. Many people also have a preferred sense of representation. One of those senses is used more than the others when we talk about our experiences. So you may notice people who are more visual tend to use more visual language and the same with those that are auditory or kinesthetic.

Consider this conversation with a husband and his wife in a therapy room:

Therapist: "So Mrs. Smith what seems to be the problem?"

Mrs. Smith: "It's my husband, he never *sees* my *point of view*, I am always trying to *show him* what I mean but he doesn't *notice* the little things. He doesn't *look* at me the same way anymore either, plus I wish he would show me his love for me".

Therapist: "Ok, Mr. Smith, what do you have to say about this?"

Mr. Smith: "I *tell* my wife that I love her, however I don't feel that she *listens* to me in general. I am always trying to *say* nice things and its like she doesn't want her to *hear* what I am trying to *tell* her"

Okay, while that script may not be worthy of an Oscar for Best Screenplay, it is an example of an easily solvable communication issue between a couple. In this scenario, the wife is more of a visual person; she wants to *see* acts of love. On the other hand, the husband is very auditory, and *says* he loves his wife and feels like he is *saying* the right things, but it is not getting across.

A situation like this can be bridged by each person using the other's representational system more. If the husband used more language that matched her "system" he could have a more fulfilling relationship. For example if he were to say to her: "I finally *see* what you mean, and I will try and *show you* my love when I say I love you, and I will *notice* more of the things you try to *show me*."

Eye contact
When a person is untrustworthy, they are more likely to look away than to look into your eyes. Therefore, creating trust and rapport is much more easily achieved when using eye contact for about 60-70% of the conversation. For a person who only establishes eye contact for about 25% of the conversation (looking away or down for the rest of the time) trust is much more difficult to establish.

A study was conducted by Cornell's Food and Brand Lab researchers using cereal boxes and the characters that are on the front of them (Cap'n

Crunch, Trix rabbit, etc.). They wanted to check if the level of eye contact of the character on the cereal box evoked more trust in the brand – basically if Cap'n Crunch was looking at you, are you more likely to trust the brand and buy it?

The participants had to look at a whole bunch of cereal boxes and rate their connection and trust to the brand. They found that people connected more when the eyes were looking at them (instead of looking down) – the results were that people felt the brand was 16% more trustworthy AND the connection was 28% higher, BECAUSE A CARTOON RABBIT LOOKED AT THEM. If a cereal box is able to create more connection and trust through eye-contact, then I believe we all have a shot!

Conclusion

Likeability has two main routes – the conscious route and the subconscious route.

Firstly the conscious route – Dr. Cialdini, in his book *Influence,* lists five ways that we create "Likeability":

1. Similarity: At its most basic level, you want to find out what a person likes, is interested in or values and relate to that.
2. Physical attractiveness: This is why attractive women are employed as models to promote products. It is also why a well-dressed presenter will often command the attention of the audience more than a scruffily-dressed presenter.
3. Compliments: We all like people who like us, and most of us like to be around people that tell us great things about ourselves. Just be careful not to over do it! Remember the 'indifference'...
4. Contact and cooperation: We tend to like people with whom we are working alongside to fulfill a common goal.
5. Conditioning and association: What car does James Bond drive? A person who I would like to be more like.

When looking at similarity – the ability to relate to a subject that the person enjoys is a great skill. A simple way to relate to a person's experience:

1. You have done that thing they are fascinated with or experienced it in some way and discuss that.
2. You have not done the thing they are speaking about but you would like to try out that experience and you talk about that.
3. You have one of those "What the hell" moments because it is something you have never heard of but get really fascinated about their fascination and ask them about it.
4. You don't even want to try and relate, so you swiftly move on to the next subject and look for 1-4.

Here are the ways in which we are able to create subconscious rapport:

- Matching And mirroring body language.
- Matching tone of voice
- Matching pace of speaking
- Matching a person's modalities
- Eye contact

Get my FREE guide – 11 Hypnotic Power words of Persuasion: Discover hot words used by hypnotists that you can start using in the next 47 minutes to make your everyday communication more persuasive

http://www.muneer.com/powerwords/

VALUE

"Value-first is a perception. If your customer does not perceive it as value, then it's not very valuable." - Jeffrey Gitomer

People are always interested in gaining items they consider valuable, and they are willing to exchange money, time or their services in order to gain something THEY consider to be worth it. People often make the mistake of assuming that a person takes action to buy an item because it is the lowest price.

A simple question will prove that this is simply not true. Let us imagine for a moment that I offered you two cars:

1. The first car is a standard cheap white tiny four door sedan, the back seats of which are meant to fit three people but, you know that if one large person got in there and sat down there would be no room for you! I am talking about the type of car that you would be scared to sneeze around because you have a feeling that it may fall over.
Now, I would offer this car to you for $150.
OR
2. Instead I offer you a super luxurious, spacious, touchscreen-enabled, does-everything-you-want (even the dishes), car. A car that is so fancy it has one of those super posh computer English-accented voices. What if I offered this second car to you for $160?

Everyone I have asked this question of in my seminars has said that they would go for the more expensive car. This is simply because when price is not a limiting factor and I have stacked the items of universal value to one side, people will go to the area where the value is stacked.
Now to be fair, this is an extreme and rather unlikely example, and

in real life there would be a much bigger price gap in those two examples. However, that bigger price gap exists because of the principle of value, which states that people are willing to give more to receive more.

"Price is what you pay, value is what you get." – Warren Buffet

While this example builds and stacks items that most people will universally hold valuable, the reality is that, just like beauty, value is in the eye of the beholder. Let's look at an example: There is a painting by Mark Rothko called Violet, Green and Red (Sorry, I can't place the image here because of the copyright fairies of the universe who may turn me into a frog for showing you an image that you can just as easily find on Google image search).

Now, I apologize to anyone in the artistic community who may be offended by the following statement, but this painting is basically just three lines, painted in the aforementioned colors. THREE LINES! And recently a Russian billionaire by the name of Dmitry Rybolovlev paid $186 *million* dollars for it. For three colored lines... Personal feelings aside, this example paints a clear picture (No pun intended. Well ok, there was a bit of intention...) of how different people place different value on things. One admirer of art may appreciate the effort that goes into pieces of work, while others are more into the statement the art may make, and so on.

Just like the beauty in art is subjective and differs from person to person – so is value.

For example, I am a person that likes to travel and I fly very often. On a short-haul flight which is less than one or two hours long, I am less concerned with the food, whether the seat reclines or if the airplane has in-flight entertainment, and so I am less concerned with which airline I am flying with and I'll generally select the lowest available price for this scenario.

People use price as a determining factor when a person does not see a difference in value between the products.

When it comes to a long-haul flight, however, I become a lot more picky. For example, next month I will be taking a 12-hour flight to the US in order to attend a seminar by Dr. Richard Bandlar (the co-creator of NLP). In this scenario, I am definitely willing to pay more and fly Business Class so that I can get in-flight entertainment, a fully-reclining seat (so I can fly later and save costs on a hotel room) while getting a good meal. I also find value in that it allows me to work in a comfortable environment up in the air and even gives me space to film some great videos for my social media channels*.

*(I have an online motivational video series called "The Mighty Mindset", which contains videos filmed up in the air in Business Class, along with videos filmed in various countries around the world. I tend to use my surroundings as metaphors to deliver messages that are more powerful than just delivering them in a mundane setting like an office. To see these videos you can subscribe to my channel at Youtube.com/Muneer)

The point is that because I see multiple elements of value here, I am willing to pay more to get a more spacious seat in Business Class. However, not everyone will find that it is worth that price justification for various reasons. If you have a whole family travelling, for example, that might change things.

When it comes down to using the "value" principle in your persuasion efforts, the most important thing to do is understand what a person actually considers "valuable", and use that to move them towards taking action.

To give you a more illustrative example, let us consider the act of getting someone to stop a bad habit like smoking using hypnotherapy, which can be a much tougher element of persuasion than the act of getting someone to buy something. After all, when you are talking about changing a habit that people have had for years, or even decades, then these are deep rooted changes that need to take place.

After studying hypnosis, hypnotherapy and NLP, I decided to specialize in helping people stop smoking. The reason that a quit smoking CD is not as effective as a one-on-one session with a coach is because everyone has different values and different reasons for wanting to quit. This is why I believe many people don't experience success when they see an amateur hypnotherapist about quitting smoking, because the hypnotist may be reading from a standardized script that may not be suitable for everyone.

In order to have an effective outcome with regards to making a person quit smoking, it is important to sit with a person and understand all their major values, their main reasons for quitting and how it will affect them for the better.

What people hold valuable changes from person to person. For some it is health, for others it is family, though I've even heard of situations where people are more concerned with their teeth than anything else. Even if a person's value was to quit so that they can impress a person of the opposite sex, that is their value, and during hypnosis the technique is to keep feeding the person's values back to them in the context of quitting.

When it comes to presenting a new idea, product or service, how do you educate a person about value when they are new to the concept? One way to establish value in an idea, product, service or action is to understand what is important to the individual (what are their values) and relate the idea, product, service or action to their value.

Earlier I mentioned how this technique is used in getting people to make huge changes like quitting smoking. It is also an important step when a salesperson tries to sell a car, because if someone is looking for a safe car for the whole family, then the salesman will have more luck if he presents a suitable car that satisfies the client's needs, and the more a person re-enforces their values while he is selling, the more successful he will be.

In the above example, the value to the shopper is quite obvious (a safe family car in this case), however sometimes a person doesn't know what they want when they are shopping around and it is important for a salesperson to try and establish what a person wants before offering random cars.

The way to establish the value is simply through questioning, for example:

Salesman: "What sort of car are you looking for today?"

Customer: "I'm not really sure."

Salesman: "Are you looking for something for yourself or for the family?"

Customer: "For myself."

Salesman, "Ok great, and are you a person that is looking for something economical or sporty?"

By gaining this information (and a lot of it), not only will the salesperson be able to show the relevant car but also be able to feed back that information to the customer when he shows him the car, e.g. "This is the perfect car for individuals who like performance and style, etc."

The second way to establish value in a product or service is through comparison. According to Professor William Poundstone, author of the book *Priceless: the myth of fair value*, he says, "Most of us are clueless about the concept of value".

There have been many experiments conducted which ultimately indicate that we will rely on whatever information that we have available to us at the time of purchase in order to make a decision. Therefore, if you are able to skew the available information at the time of purchase, then you can sway a person's decision.

Many a restaurant in various parts of the world use this pricing strategy when it comes to how much they charge for wine. They know that the average person does not know how much different wine bottles cost, nor are they able to really distinguish the taste between the different varieties of wine. Since wine prices vary significantly from cheap to very high in price, they are able to exploit this fact to their advantage.

Therefore, most menus will place three different price choices of wine, for example:

- A $10 bottle
- A $35 bottle
- A $70 bottle

In the above scenario, the objective of the restaurant is to sell the $35 option. It has been discovered that most people will look at the three and say they don't want to get the cheapest available option, however the most expensive is a little pricey, and therefore they select the middle option.

In actual fact, the most expensive option is placed there to make the middle option look affordable, while the lower-priced option is placed there in order to make the mid-ranged one seem significantly better, but within reach. The average restaurant goer simply picks the bottle of wine based on the price and nothing else. If only the cheapest option was offered, then they may just select that. However the cheapest and most expensive bottles are both offered in order to sell the mid-priced bottle, which will likely boast by far the biggest profit margin!

To support this theory, a study was conducted to show just how much the information that is available at the time of purchase can influence a decision. A behavioral economist by the name of Dan Ariely was intrigued by the pricing structure that was created by an advert that has run in *The Economist* magazine. In the advertising campaign, which was designed to sell subscriptions to their magazine, the economist offered three different packages:

- A web-only subscription to their magazine for $59;
- A print-only subscription to their magazine for $125;
- And a web-and-print subscription which was also offered for $125.

Dan Ariely was so fascinated with this structure that, using his students, he ran a test to see what the outcome should be. In the first test he offered them the exact options as they were stated, and 16% opted for the $59 web-only package with 84% opting in for the web-and-print subscription. 0% opted for the print-only package.

Type of subscription	Price of subscription	% of people to select it
Web-only	$59	16%
Print-only	$125	0%
Web-and-print	$125	84%

He then repeated the poll, however this time he only offered people two options: the web-only and the web-and-print. This time, 68% of people went with web-only and 32% had gone for web-and-print.

Type of subscription	Price of subscription	% of people to select it
Web-only	$59	68%
Web-and-print	$125	32%

So basically, by removing this seemingly useless bit of information, they changed the revenue generated by a huge amount!

Conclusion:

- People have different concepts of value – the ability to identify what a person values and using that in your communication will make you much more efficient at getting results.
- The concept of finding out what people want and feeding that back to them is extremely simple. However, it is very efficiently used to get people to make huge long term changes in hypnosis.
- People do not generally have a benchmark system of what prices are for most items, so they compare the closest readily available information in order to determine value.

- By adjusting the closest readily available information you can allow people to determine better value in your products.

Interested in seeing the videos that I create up in the air?

Subscribe to my YouTube Channel at Youtube.com/Muneer

OTHER PEOPLE'S PERCEPTIONS – O.P.P.

"Most people live their life around what other people do." - Tom Scholz

I have actually done it – I've taken an early 90's explicit rap song and molded it into a title for a serious chapter in my book. These are the little joys of writing a book and coming up with your own model! I don't exactly need to be overly prim and proper ☺, I can use smiley faces and be naughty by nature (I really hope somebody gets that reference!).

However, the topic of "OPP" in this book (and in my model) relates to how the perception of other people plays into your persuasion efforts and how it can affect a person's decision process. There are ultimately four main forms of OPP:

- What other people are doing;
- What other people are saying;
- How other people perceive authority;
- Consistency with what we communicate to others.

'Other people's perceptions' is a subject that is very relevant, especially today with the growth of social media and the digital world. To give you an example of what I mean: I have always loved to watch TV and movies. I am also fortunate enough to have a wide selection of cinemas close to my home and I have an on-demand television service that allows me to browse through many different options of things to watch.

I often scroll through these options trying to decide what to watch (unless my daughter is around, in which case I am fairly restricted to watching Princess Sofia). On the rare occasion that the choice is purely mine, when I'm browsing and I happen to come across a film I have not heard of, I go to the IMDb website or app on my phone and check it out. IMDb stands for Internet Movie Data Base, and it lists almost every movie and television show on Earth, with ratings from people all over the world. One of the website's features is that both critics and the general public can rate and review the movies or TV shows, and the average rating for a movie is listed on the site.

When I am researching a movie that I have not heard of, I check a couple of things on IMDb:

1. How many people have voted for that movie? If loads of people have gone to see it then that is definitely a great sign. This relates to the first point of OPP: What other people are doing.

2. What are other people saying about it? If thousands of people have said they like the movie, then the chances that I will like it are definitely going to be high. This obviously relates to the second point: What other people are saying.

3. Finally, since the IMDb website is considered an authoritative source of movie stats (mainly because it is such a large aggregator of information), I will trust the score more fully. This relates to the third point: How other people perceive it.

In case you're not a movie fan, let me give you another example. Tripadvisor is a website that does the same for travel. As an avid traveler I will spend time on the website and check hotel reviews, tour reviews and look up activities to do if I am visiting a city for the first time.

The fourth principle of OPP – what we say to others – just means that we are likely to stay consistent in what we tell other people. Therefore, if we have gone onto one of these sites and voted favorably for a movie, then we are more likely to maintain our position if we are asked in the future.

These websites are all examples of three of the elements of OPP in action, and an example of the fourth if we ourselves participate. Other People's Perceptions can be extremely powerful and valuable, because we generally like to take the simple route in situations and defer our judgment to what others are thinking and doing or having an authority tell us to do something.

Let us look at each of the principles of OPP a little more closely:

WHAT OTHER PEOPLE ARE DOING

Allow me to give you an amusing example: A social experiment was conducted in which a woman goes to what seems like a doctor's surgery waiting room. In this waiting room are a bunch of actors posing as waiting patients. Every few minutes a beeping noise comes on and all the actors have been informed to stand up for a moment then to sit down.

The unsuspecting lady sees people stand up the first time the beeping noise sounds and looks around wondering what the hell is going on. On only the third time round she hesitates but then doesn't want to be the only odd one out, so she stands up too! She then continues to do so as the beeping sound comes on every few minutes and while she is waiting one by one all the actors are called into the doctor's office. Then hilariously this woman is alone in the waiting room, and yet still stands every time she hears the beeping sound even though she is on her own.

Here is where it gets interesting – a new gentleman comes to the waiting room who is also not an actor. He initially has the same reaction as the lady when she first started by getting a little confused. However on the second beep he decides to join her and follow the norm that seems to have been established.

Slowly but surely more and more people come to the waiting room, none of whom are actors, and sure enough all of them are standing up for the beep every few minutes, and none of them question the process, despite the fact that they don't have any clue as to why they are doing it in the first place.

(You can find a video of this social experiment on my blog at this address: http://www.muneer.com/experimentopp/)

This social experiment shows the power of the first area of OPP – what other people are doing. When we see everyone else doing something we are more likely to do something ourselves. This can sometimes be dangerous too – a crowd of people that are irritated and disgruntled can start to get out of hand very quickly and cause individuals in the group to do things that they wouldn't normally do that they may regret later – a phenomenon known as 'mob mentality'.
I have spoken in the first chapter about how I was bullied when I was younger. The crazy thing is that there were a few people in the group who were friendly enough to me on a one-on-one basis. However, when part of a group they followed the pattern of what everyone else was doing.

On a corporate level, the retail industry has used the principle of OPP for years to persuade shoppers to buy products. When major department stores have big sales, they allow the crowds to develop and a massive queue to form outside the store, because this creates the illusion that everyone wants what is on sale, which in turn makes more people want it.

Brands like Apple, Playstation and even movie franchises like Star Wars have used a combination of "Scarcity" (from the Fear of Loss principle) and "what other people are doing" (from the OPP principle) to launch new products amazingly successfully.

They create limited quantities of their products during the launch phase which are only available for the select group of lucky people on a first-come-first-served basis. This incites people to queue up outside the store overnight, thus communicating to the world: "LOOK at how many people want this, and what they are willing to do to get it!"

It would be easy to assume that the queues have nothing to do with persuasion and that people are generally only interested in the product. However, to understand the power of a queue on the perceptions of people all you need to do is hear a story told by Dr. Cialdini in his book *Influence,* who recounts the story of a bank crisis in Singapore a number of years ago.

One day a number of people were standing by a bus stop in Singapore. On this particular day there was a bus strike, and as a result a large crowd started to form at the bus stop. As this crowd continued to grow, it seemed to passersby that the crowds were waiting for the bank nearby to open, prompting fears that something was wrong with the bank and people's money may be at risk!

Soon the word spread, which drew bigger crowds of people who joined the group of people waiting for the bank to open. The bigger the crowd grew, the more attention it attracted, until there was a massive crowd outside the bank anxiously waiting for it to open so that they could 'save their money'. When the bank's staff showed up for the day, they were surprised and shocked by the unexpected mob that rushed in to withdraw all their money, nearly causing a cash crisis for the bank.

It took a while for the bank executives to understand what had happened and the reasons for the sudden rush, and after some investigation involving interviews with people involved and CCTV footage, they found that it was all linked to this simple principle of OPP, and 'what other people are doing'.

When I did door-to-door sales, the sales executives used to refer to this principle as "the Jones theory" based on the phrase "Keeping up with the Joneses". This is a term where everyone in a neighborhood would adopt a behavior based on what all the other neighbors were doing. For door-to-door sales this was actually a very relevant phrasing of the principle and something I learned to use extensively.

For example, after I had signed up "Mrs. Cliffords" on a street, when I would go down to the next few houses I would say, "I have actually just finished registering your neighbor Mrs. Cliffords...". They may or may not know Mrs. Cliffords personally, but the reason I made the statement was to illustrate that their neighbors were signing up. If they *did* happen to know her, my chances of signing up the new person multiplied. Once I got a second signup I would then use both names the next time I spoke to someone.

As a side note, I believe in integrity and that you should always tell the truth. Therefore I would only use a person's name if they had actually signed up. If I had not yet signed anyone up that day, I would say, "The reason people are doing this... etc." Which would be true as well since people were signing up, I just didn't have a specific name at that point.

Using this principle also came in handy in the handling of objections, for example when someone would say to me, "I am not sure if this is for me!" I would turn over the objections using multiple persuasion principles listed in the book, especially the concept of "What other people are doing".

So, for example, my reply would be, "I completely understand what you are saying. In fact Mrs. Cliffords (OPP) initially felt the same way. What she then found out is that the reason most other people are doing it (OPP) is because of the value today's offer has (Value) and since we are only here today (Fear of loss/urgency) she signed up so she wouldn't lose out, and I'm sure you wouldn't want to miss out too (Fear of loss), would you? So shall I put this in your name or your husbands name?"

The previous example relies heavily on the principles of persuasion, though it also uses a couple of other techniques: obliterating objections, the 'Double-Bind Close' (from my consistent conversion phase) and an example of a 'Minor Yes Set' (another set from the patterns of persuasion), all of which are taught in my wider program and in the Invincible Influence system that I describe at the end of the book.

Let us now turn our attention to the second area of "OPP": What other people are saying. This can also be summarized as, "Other people can sell you better than you can sell yourself!"

Picture this: You are at a function full of close friends, and one of your friends comes up and starts telling everyone how he went to the most awesome restaurant two nights ago, the service was amazing, the food was unlike anything he had eaten before and the view, oh man, his camera just didn't do it justice.

Now contrast this with an advert from the restaurant saying, "Amazing food, Amazing Service & Amazing Views – Come visit us today!"

Most people are subjected to these ads on a daily basis, and yet pay them no attention. According to a study conducted by brand assessment specialists Nielsen, 83% of online respondents in 60 countries say they trust the recommendations of friends and family, making it the most credible and effective form of advertising. While this last example relates to friends and family, which is the most powerful, having a stranger (who has nothing to gain) recommend something can be very powerful too.

In my earlier example, I asked you to imagine that it was a good friend talking about the restaurant. Now imagine that you are a guest at the function and you hear someone that you don't know tell his friends how he went to the most awesome restaurant two nights ago, the service was amazing, the food was unlike anything he had eaten before and the view... etc.

If you heard it from a person who you know has nothing to gain from recommending the restaurant, then you will very likely be intrigued, yet if you saw exactly the same message in an advert from the restaurant, you probably wouldn't pay any attention.

There are many businesses that are solely built on this principle alone. For example, I work closely with therapists, consultants and trainers, and my initial product, "The Client Creation Formula", was designed to support those people in getting more clients. In the process of creating my product, I interviewed a number of coaches and therapists who all had successful practices, and asked them where they found many of their clients. The overwhelming majority said referrals were their main source of new clients. This means that their #1 source of business was "what people are saying"!

When I had my home business promoting personal development products, I would often present the benefits of my program and invite people that had signed up with me previously to come and speak about how the product had benefited them in their lives. So that begs the question: How is this useful when "I" am trying to persuade someone and I am alone?

After all if I am in the process of speaking to someone, what use is someone else saying something if they are not there at the time? The ideal situation would be to have people that follow us around everywhere singing our praises on demand, which isn't a very practical solution (believe me I have looked into it ☺). So, lets look at the next best things.

Recording people for official sales material:
If you are actually in the process of selling yourself in a professional aspect, if you have a website, sales letter or even a brochure, then write down their quote with a picture, or show a recording of a person in a video. Ask people to give you a testimonial and display this to others. Many websites and sales letters already use this technique for a reason – because it works!

Letters:
Some therapists ask clients to send them a letter after three months when they have successfully achieved their desired outcome. For example, I would ask a person to send me a letter after 3 months of not smoking letting me know how they have gotten on. I also obtain permission for me to use these letters. You can then show them to interested people, saying, "I actually just received this letter from one of my clients a little while ago and she

was extremely happy with the work we had done together."

During my door-to-door sales days, after a visit I would often have to ask people to fill out a survey stating they were happy with the service. I would often suggest something like, "Oh, and if you were happy with me personally then please feel free to say something nice and funny about me, it would really help me look good in front of my boss... you don't have to say I'm good looking although that may help too!" People always love a bit of humor, and I somehow managed to get people to say I was good looking on a number of my review forms in the end!

I would then go from house to house with multiple review sheets that said positive things about me, and I could use these in a conversation as a quote or, if it wasn't sensitive information, I may just show the little note. For example, I may be speaking with someone who was a little annoyed with receiving different people at their door, and I would often say something like, "I completely understand that you have loads of people knocking on your door, however they probably aren't as charming as me – even Mrs. Cliffords said so – in fact this is what she said (taking out the piece of paper), 'Muneer was respectable and professional and I enjoyed speaking to him... and he is good looking.'" As a joke I would then whisper, "I think maybe Mrs Cliffords has a crush on me!" which would most likely get a bit of a smile along with earning a few moments with the person.

In the absence of recorded material or proof, just quoting people is still very effective – after all you are not the person that said it. For example I tend not to like speaking about my conversational hypnosis skills, however one of the guys I trained with, Ricardo Moya, actually recorded a video after I had done some work with him at a seminar, and in the video he actually says, "I was blown away with Muneer's ability to use conversational hypnosis, he is a good... *very* good hypnotist." When I saw the video he recorded I nearly blushed (although I was unable to since I am too dark), but I must say I was so humbled by what he said.

Now, I would like you to read that last paragraph as if I were relating it to you in person. By saying those things out loud in a conversational style, I would be able to come across as humble while speaking about my skills and quoting a testimonial.

Remember: only state things that are true. We have all had people say good things about us at one point or another in our lives, so just find something that you can use. As a side note, quoting people in conversations can be used for multiple purposes and is expanded upon much further in a technique called "that's what they said", which is a part of the "patterns of persuasion" phase in the wider *Invincible Influence* system.

This brings us to the next point of the "Other People's Perceptions - OPP" Model:

HOW OTHER PEOPLE PERCEIVE AUTHORITY

This is a complicated way of saying that people are much more likely to trust an authority figure telling them what to do versus an amateur giving them instructions. We are taught to respect and follow authority from when we are young – even rebels who disrespect traditional authority respect the authority within their social groups or peer networks!

In our society, uniforms are used as clear indicators of authority, so when we hear instructions from those people we will most likely follow them. When I see a uniformed person at an airport telling me to take off my shoes I take them off, no matter how stinky my feet are! I'm an Arab – I tend not to argue in airports...

This is the same if I see a uniformed policeman who asks me to do something, a white-coated doctor that tells me not to eat something, or if I saw a person in army fatigues telling me I can't go down a certain road – like most people I would most likely comply.

The dependency on authority can often be powerful and excessive. For example, in the medical journal *Medication Errors: Causes and Prevention*, a number of cases were identified by Temple University professors where errors have been made in the field of medicine because a pharmacist or nurse received instructions from a doctor that should have been questioned (they should have known better). However, because it came from a source of authority they did not feel it was their place to question.

Con-artists try and use the title 'General' often in their scam emails for this reason. However, since the notion of a random army General writing to you after just happening to find your email to propose a business venture from his random email account is so ludicrous that it deserves no trust or credibility, sort of like the email I received from MrsMichelleObama206@yahoo.co.uk, where she wanted to give me lots and lots of money from her husband. For some reason I didn't go for it, and that had more to do with my belief of the email than my belief of her! If I met her and she said, "Here take some money," I would just say "Thank you," take the money, and walk away.

So the question is, how do you establish authority if you do not have an authoritative title or a uniform? The air of authority is created by a number of different things:

- Your title: President, CEO, Senior So-and-So etc., all of these create an air of authority.
- How you dress: Although uniforms are an obvious example of establishing authority, your suit can establish your authority, but also hurt it. Did you know that even the color of your tie can have an emotional effect on a person? For example, a solid red tie worn with a dark suit can communicate passion, knowing what you want and confidence. Did you ever wonder why politicians wear solid red or blue ties? These are power colors.
- Your surroundings: The place in which you are conducting business, the car you are driving or the people you are surrounded with.
- Your achievements: Writing a book, making a film, giving a talk – any of these would establish yourself as an authority.
- What others say about you: Mentioned previously, however something you must be aware of.

To illustrate the power this part of the principle plays on us, consider the following example: In 1974 Stanley Milgram, a psychologist at Yale University, published the results of an experiment is his study "Obedience to Authority: An Experimental View". They took your everyday average person and put them in a lab, and some guys in white coats came and said to them, "We are going to ask a respondent in the other room a number of questions. If they get the answer wrong, we would like you to flip these switches to give them an electric shock. Every time you shock them, go up to the next switch, where the voltage will go up by 15 volts for the next shock."

There were 30 switches, and they even had a scale indicating how high the shocks would go. More alarming was the wording that they used next to the levels (see the figure below).

Slight shock/Moderate shock/Strong shock/Very strong shock/Intense shock/Extreme intensity shock/Danger: Severe shock/XXX (Yes, that was the label!)

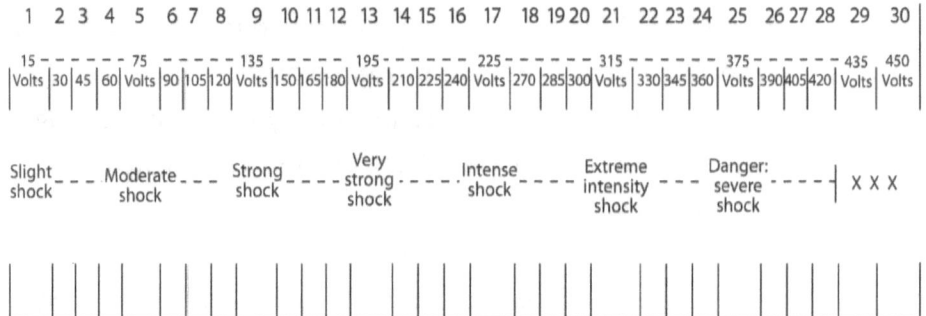

*The labelling on the machine that the participants used to deliver shocks.

Now the shocks were actually not real, and the respondents being asked the questions by the experimenters were actually actors. They started out by acting out discomfort, and slowly moving on to screaming and demands to be let go. In the event that there was any hesitation by those administering the shocks, the experimenters would offer one of these pre-produced phrases:

"Please continue." Or, "Please go on."

"The experiment requires that you continue."

"It is absolutely essential that you continue."

"You have no other choice, you must go on."

The crazy thing is that, because people in white lab coats told them to, 65% of the participants kept on going and gave them the whole enchilada – 450 volts! At this point, the actors were feigning being close to death, but the participants kept going. This is really a shocking (see what I did there?) example of how far people are willing to go for an authority figure.

And finally, let us take a look at:

CONSISTENCY WITH WHAT WE COMMUNICATE TO OTHERS

This is essentially where people are much more likely to remain consistent based on things that they have done, said or written down previously. The experiment I mention earlier has a definite element of consistency because the people are remaining consistent to what they have been doing, which is following the authority person's orders.

When my wife gets upset over something that she says is important, she will remain consistent with what she has said! (Did I mention that she inspired me to learn hypnosis, in the vain hope that I may get her to change her mind one day?)

Derren Brown produced a very real and scary documentary called *Pushed to the Edge,* in which this principle of OPP is put to use to see if people will commit the extreme act of pushing someone off of a roof. The documentary starts with an unwitting participant being filmed at a location that has been rigged with multiple hidden cameras. The person being tested is completely unaware that this is a staged event and that he is being filmed.

Over time he is given small requests that gradually increase in intensity by a person of relative authority. These requests start off small in nature, for example placing vegetarian flags on sausage rolls. Over the course of a number of hours, though, they increase in severity and soon the person being filmed finds himself so deep on the path that they are unable to turn back. I won't tell you how this ends so that you can watch it yourself. However, the experiment has been so elaborately and cleverly designed that it's able to actually get a normal person to the point where they would even consider pushing someone off of a building!

While there was some controversy surrounding the experiment in terms of pushing a person towards that point, the objective of pointing out the power these principles have on us was certainly communicated. According to Dr. Cialdini, "Once we have made a choice or taken a stand, we will encounter personal and interpersonal pressures to behave consistently with that commitment. Those pressures will cause us to respond in ways that justify our earlier decision."

There was an experiment done in 1966 that appeals to my door-to-door experience, where Jonathan Freedman and Scott Fraser examined something that they called the "foot in the door" technique. In the experiment a couple of researchers went round asking people to put up a large billboard in the front of their yards urging people to 'Drive Carefully'. One person found that only 17% of people actually agreed. The other researcher went around to different homes and found that a much higher figure of 76% of people agreed to his request!

Why was this?

Simple – the second researcher had gone to people's houses who had been previously contacted and who had agreed to place a small three-inch display up in their window that read: "Be a safe driver".

It was a small and reasonable request that suddenly became a much larger one. Those people in the first group had only been contacted once, and so this initial request was too large and too soon.

HOW DO WE USE THIS ELEMENT OF CONSISTENCY IN PERSUASION?

There is a principle commonly taught in sales, NLP and hypnosis called a 'yes set'. This essentially states that you are more likely to get someone to agree to something once they have been put into a pattern of agreement.

Let me demonstrate: I would like you to say the word "Silk" to yourself 20 times very quickly.

I know this is a book but do it anyway. Go on, no one is looking – you don't even have to say it out loud! It will be worth it...

Ok I am going to trust that you have done so, and if you have let me ask you a question:

What do cows drink?

If you answered "Milk", then in you would, in fact, be wrong, because cows produce milk, but drink water. However when our brain gets into a pattern, it remains consistent with that pattern.

Therefore, getting someone to agree to something big can come about by getting them to agree consistently to smaller items that grow in size. Think of it this way – despite my amazingly good looks, I would not be able to go up to a woman on the streets and ask her to marry me. Among other things, it is way too sudden, in her eyes it is way too soon, and my wife would kill me way too violently!

However, people do meet and get married all the time, but they require smaller incremental agreements: agree to say hello, agree to exchange names, agree to talk, agree to exchange contact details and so on. Every major agreement is made up of a consistent number of smaller micro-agreements.

CONCLUSION:

There are ultimately four main forms of Other People's Perception (OPP):

- What other people are doing
- What other people are saying
- How other people perceive authority
- Consistency with what we communicate to others

What other people are doing: We are more likely to do something that we see others as doing.

What other people are saying: We are more likely to follow the recommendations of others who we regard as indifferent to the product.

How we perceive authority: We are wired to follow authority figures and respect people that we consider experts. Even anti-authority figures like to follow an anti-authority leader!

Consistency: We are more likely to act consistently with how we communicate to others – this can be used powerfully in persuasion by bringing about a yes set, for example, which establishes a consistent pattern of agreement.

Would you like to learn how to create a hypnotic "Yes set"?

When you subscribe for my FREE guide – "11 Hypnotic Power words of Persuasion" you will also receive details on how you can learn to create powerful yes sets.

http://www.muneer.com/powerwords/

RECIPROCITY

"Take time to appreciate employees and they will reciprocate in a thousand ways." - Bob Nelson

Recently I did a talk where I walked up to the audience members and asked them to pay me a certain amount of money. The audience laughed and smiled and although no-one paid (insert sad face here) it piqued their curiosity. I then asked everyone if they were to take my request for payment seriously, what question would be on their mind? They all unanimously said, "What for?"

This is because, as a generality, when we give something to someone, we expect something in return. Most cultures and societies all over the world are trained in the rules of give and take from an early age, which is how shopping works all over the world. We give something in order to receive. The opposite, however, is also true – when we receive something, we feel like we should give back too. This is known as the Law of Reciprocity.

Also known as, "You scratch my back, and I'll scratch yours!"

Allow me to illustrate how I experience this law frequently in my life: Being in the Middle East, the UAE, where I live, serves as a very central point for travel in the world. Because I have lived in many different countries I am fortunate enough to know people from all the world who, at some point or other, travel to (or via) the UAE since two of the major global airlines Emirates and Etihad operate from there.

Now I have a strange activity that I really enjoy – I love being a tour guide. I enjoy this for a number of reasons:
1. I travel a lot and enjoy going on tours in various parts of the

world myself.

2. When you contribute to a person's experience while they travel, you become a very memorable person in their lives.

3. I love making people happy whilst educating them.

4. I love showing people the region I am from. While technically I am from Oman, which is the country next door, the cultures are very similar.

5. I am also passionate about shattering misconceptions towards Arabs and Muslims. Therefore, I love showing people who are first setting foot in the Arab world that even though the media doesn't want you to know it, most Gulf countries are actually some of the safest, most developed and cosmopolitan places in the world – a stark contrast to what many imagine from their run-ins with the media and random blogs written by people that have never actually visited the place!

I love shattering misconceptions, and when a person has this image in the back of their minds of sand, tents, camels and random huts, and then you show them the world's tallest building, a Formula 1 track that goes through a hotel, Ferraris as police cars, a nightlife that rivals some of the greatest cities in the world and beautiful, fashionable people from all corners of the globe wearing whatever fashion they want, that kind of shatters their misconceptions in a big way.

So, when I learn that someone I know is visiting the country, whether a friend, acquaintance or friend of a friend, I take it upon myself to try and show them around, because I like to do it. I never do this with any expectation of anything in return – I do this because I enjoy it (what I get in return is feeling good about it!).

In most cases I am never likely to need anything in return. However, because I do tend to travel often, I have come across a time or two where I have traveled to a country in which lives a person I've shown around my hometown. When that happens, I will reach out and let that person know that I will be visiting their area. Sometimes this can occur three or four years after they have visited.

While I only reach out to let people know I am visiting and that it would be good to see them, I am always pleasantly surprised by the level of hospitality I am offered in a country – I have been fortunate to have enjoyed personalized tours from local friends in many new countries and cities, and have experienced some pretty spectacular things around the world. My travels have been so amazing because I have experienced friends going out of their way to look after me and ensure that I have everything I need in a new city/country.

The reason I so readily get these offers is because of this law of reciprocity. As individuals we want to do things for people that have done something for us. It is human nature to give back! While this seems like a purely theoretical concept, it has actually been measured. In the book *Influence* by Dr. Cialdini, he talks about a study that was conducted in New York where they worked with waiters/waitresses in order to measure the change in tips when mints were given by the waiting staff along with the bill.

The study started out by establishing a baseline for the amount of tips received when the bill was given with no added gifts. They then looked at the average increase in tips if one mint was added to the bill plate. Tips in this scenario went up by 3%. Next they looked at the average increase in tips if two mints were added – this saw a 14% increase in the average tip. However, the biggest increase was when they saw a waiter/ waitress give a mint, begin to walk away then come back, look at the people and say, "For you lovely people here is an extra mint." This scenario saw a whopping 23% increase in tips, since they felt the waiter/ waitress was doing something for them personally and therefore wanted to reciprocate.

We like to give back to people that give things to us. This law of reciprocity can therefore be used to your advantage in the game of sales, influence and persuasion. Jeff Walker, who created the Product Launch Formula, a way of selling your educational products online for large sums of money in short spaces of time, has taught many people to do this successfully. So successfully, in fact, that many of the largest multi-million dollar product launches that have happened online have followed this formula. These are launches that have generated $2-4 million dollars in a matter of one week.

How have they done this? By using many of the principles of persuasion very effectively. However, one of the major cornerstones of this has been offering a free video series that offers immense value. This would typically consist of three videos released over a period of time that really help to solve three major problems for a person, and the content, freely given, would typically be of such great value that a person says to themselves, "If their free stuff is this good, their paid stuff must be amazing!"

I, myself have run free seminars where I have not charged a penny for attendance. I then make sure it is better than any other paid seminar out there. As a result, when I offer people the opportunity to train with me at the end, people are excited and much keener on the prospect than if I would have asked them to pay to train with me right at the start.

Because I give great value, and people see the quality of my seminars as well as the application of the knowledge, they are also willing to pay a higher price than some of the other less-premium courses out there. This concept doesn't just work with the larger deals – it also works with everyday consumables as well. The reason supermarkets often give free samples is because they want to activate this little sensation of wanting to repay the debt.

One of the first and most famous manifestations of the principle of reciprocity was when a social psychologist by the name of Dennis T Regan from Cornell University conducted a study in 1971 entitled "Effects of a favor and liking on compliance", which was published in the Journal of Experimental Psychology. (I like using sentences like that – they show I do my homework!)

In the experiment, the participants were told that they were there to examine art in which they would be looking into reproductions of paintings. Secretly they were checking to see how doing a person a favor would alter how they behaved when asked to do something later on. They had two participants at a time in the room doing the exercise – the subject of the experiment, and an examiner who was disguised as a subject. The undercover examiner would leave the room at some point, and in half the cases he would return with two cans of coke.

He would then say, "I asked him (the overseer) if I could get myself a coke, and he said it was ok, so I bought one for you too!" After this, he would return to work and refuse any money offered in return. Later on, the undercover subject would reach out to the other participant to let him know that he has raffle tickets that he is selling to raise money for his high school gym. He would ask the participant if he/she would be interested in buying some raffle tickets for $0.25 each. What they discovered was that the group who had received the coke from the undercover examiner purchased twice the number of raffle tickets than the group who did not receive anything. This group also paid far more for raffle tickets than the value of the coke!

I find it interesting how people apply this research when they read it. Many people want to put it into action in their sales and persuasion efforts, and some social psychologists want to push the barrier. In 1976, Dr. Phil Kunz, a sociology professor at Brigham University, wanted to test this out and see how far he could push the reciprocity factor.

As an experiment, he sent out 578 Christmas cards to a sample of complete strangers and random people he didn't know. He got 117 replies! That is, 117 cards from people that he didn't know, some of who had even included long letters and pictures of family. Only six of the respondents actually admitted that they didn't know the guy.

A number of years ago, I was named by Arabian Business Magazine as one of the Top 10 Arabs on Twitter – I was outranked by Sheikh Mohammed Al Maktoum, the ruler of Dubai, and Queen Rania of Jordan, among others... And I'll be very honest: I was kind of ok with them beating me!

People would ask me how I got to have so many followers, and it was partly because I had reached out to so many people online first to speak with them and follow them. As a result I had many people reach back to me. I suppose this was my modern day version of what Dr. Kunz did, though I didn't pretend I knew people – I just reached out to people who were interested in my subject area and followed them first while initiating a conversation, and in turn many had followed me.

Let us shift our attention now to how there are businesses out there that will completely rely on the law of reciprocity in order to operate. On my travels I have visited many a city, and using trip-advisor I have found some of the most popular tours in many big cities are the 'Free Walking Tours'. If you have ever been on one of these tours, they are pretty awesome. You typically have a well-spoken, near theatrical individual who shows you around the city they live in and, at the end, they let you know that one of the ways that they are able to function as a business is through the generous tips and donations that they receive from others. People are not obliged to give anything, though they are grateful for whatever they receive.

Usually, as a result of spending close to four hours guiding people for free, they receive a generous amount of tips (I would say that over 90% of people on the tours donate), and moreover because so much value was given for "free" many people go onto the Internet and rate these tours very highly, allowing them to enjoy more business through the OPP principle of persuasion we spoke about earlier.

Street performers make a living from this principle too. After all, sometimes they don't even ask for money and just have a hat placed in front of their performance area indicating that they are accepting tips. In return for us being entertained, we feel obliged to contribute a payment. Because we are so aware of the reciprocity principle we will also avoid taking things from others because we do not want to have this feeling of "owing anyone anything". I used to walk around Covent Garden often while I was living in London, and this is where you'll find many street performers.

Occasionally I would be in a rush and I would notice a crowd start to develop around a street performer, and I would instantly be torn, because I was curious to see the performance (the OPP principle), but if I was in a rush I would not want to be the person who enjoyed some of their entertainment for only 30 seconds without contributing anything (collections of tips would usually happen at the end of the performance). You may have witnessed people refusing help from others, saying its because, "I don't want to feel like we owe them anything!" Perhaps you have done it yourself at some point – I know I have.

In many cultures, a guy will often attempt to approach a woman by offering to "Buy her a drink". The guy does this because he feels that based on the law of reciprocity, if he is allowed to buy her a drink, then that means that she will be obliged to have a conversation with him. Girls will also refuse to be bought a drink by a guy if they do not want to feel like they owe it to the guy to spend time with him. It is generally understood (although not universally practiced!) that a woman would not accept a drink and then ignore the man after he has enacted this purchase.

When someone does something for us and we don't give back, we don't feel as good about it because deep down inside we feel like we are breaking some unwritten law. Therefore in most situations we will avoid this like the plague. It is as though we are upsetting the balance of things and karma may come and back at us with a slap on the back of the head when we are not looking!

The power of reciprocity lies in understanding that when a person accepts something from you, they are more inclined to follow the path of least resistance. It is what makes us say yes to covering for a work friend on a weekend when we have plans, because they covered for us once upon a time.

The applications of this principle are vast and wide – the question is: how can you adapt this to fit your influence and persuasion efforts?

Get my FREE guide – 11 Hypnotic Power words of Persuasion: Discover hot words used by hypnotists that you can start using in the next 47 minutes to make your everyday communication more persuasive

http://www.muneer.com/powerwords/

THE INVINCIBLE INFLUENCE SYSTEM

"If you have a reasonable system for pursuing success, it can survive a lot of face-plants along the way. That knowledge makes success seem accessible." - Scott Adams

Influence and persuasion is an extremely vast topic, sort of like learning how to cook food. Just like cooking and its many cuisines, influence and persuasion can and does have a whole range of books on each of its focus areas.

In the same respect, there are also multiple specialties when it comes to persuasion. The cool thing is that these specialties can be placed into phases of a system that I like to call "Invincible Influence". The mastery of these phases will make you the most invincible influencer (hence the very clever name) – think of it like a super power, but without the cape, spandex and red underwear worn on the outside!

Under the Invincible Influence system - there are 5 main categories:

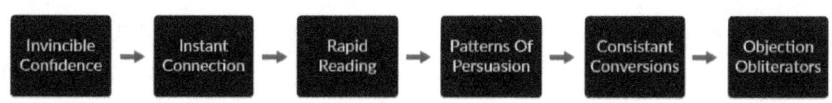

The Principles of Persuasion discussed in this book belong to the fourth phase - Patterns of Persuasion. This phase gives you a deep understanding of what it takes to persuade people, from the things that you say to how you formulate your offers, the hypnotic language patterns that you can use and more.

I have led with the persuasion principles as it is one of my favorites, this is the part that really develops a lot of your persuasion skills for many different situations. I also wanted to give you a brief understanding of the other parts of the system so that you understand how these all fit together, especially since I have referred to them throughout the book and will be releasing further books on the subject in the future.

Let me start at the first phase of the system - Invincible Confidence:

In the first chapter, I spoke about "The Persuasion Results Formula", which demonstrates that results in persuasion come based on two things: your skills and the number of people you reach.

Whether it's networking, job hunting, sales, negotiating or even dating, in every situation there is a big difference between relying on the decision of one person or many people. You are more likely achieve a better result if you speak to 10 people than only relying on one.

A major challenge, however, is that many people have a fear of approaching strangers. This phase of the Invincible Influence system is about banishing limiting beliefs, changing your associations to the meeting of people and understanding that the more people you meet, the more results you get.

(By the way – sharing "The Persuasion Results Formula" was giving you enough of the first phase so that at least at a logical level you understand the value of approaching people). I also have hypnotic recordings available at InfluenceTheory.com that can help you gain more confidence when it comes to meeting people.

The next phase of the system is Instant Connection:

Part of the fear of approaching people is also related to how you feel people will initially react when you do approach them. I want you to believe that it is actually possible to get someone to feel connected to you and to feel like they know you within a matter of a few seconds. Using cutting-edge body language signals, sub-conscious preparation and language pattern signals, it is possible to hack a person's perception into feeling like they are connected to you. Combining this with NLP techniques of rapport building, this phase is all about developing an ongoing feeling of connection and rapport.

If you're still doubting that this is possible, consider this: Have you ever walked into a room in a happy mood, but then upon seeing someone who is extremely upset, instantly your state has changed? Or, perhaps you have been on the receiving end of the technique that I am teaching, for example you were at an event where a person walked up to you, introduced themselves and you instantly thought to yourself, "That person is so charming and charismatic. I like them!" When all that person said to you was "Hi, my name is X, what's your name?"

You believe it's because that person has "a certain something", but it's important to understand that "a certain something" is something that can actually be learned.

This brings me to the next phase – Rapid Reading:

This connects the last phase with the basic concept that everyone's body has a "language" that can be read and understood once you learn how to do so. In this phase you are able to understand how a person thinks, organizes information, how best to communicate with them and what information to feed back to them.

This brings us to the Patterns of Persuasion phase – this is where the "principles of persuasion" comes into it. This whole book is dedicated to the Principles of Persuasion because it is a detailed topic that can make you an amazing influencer when you talk, when you write or when you offer something online.

This phase also includes hypnotic language patterns and yes sets.

The fifth phase is Consistent Conversions:

This phase is all about moving elegantly and effectively moving a person towards taking action in a desired direction after you have planted the seeds of persuasion.

Finally we have the Objection Obliterator phase:

This phase is simply about the most cutting-edge techniques to handle and overturn objections.

This book covers a fundamental aspect of the Invincible Influence system – the persuasion principles. This is the biggest and most important starting point on your journey to becoming a persuasion technique ninja.

Get my FREE guide – 11 Hypnotic Power words of Persuasion: Discover hot words used by hypnotists that you can start using in the next 47 minutes to make your everyday communication more persuasive

http://www.muneer.com/powerwords/

WHAT NEXT?

At this point, I have gone through the 6 principles of persuasion and have somewhat subtly* hinted that there will be more to come – in video form, live seminars and more books, Yay, more content creation for me!

*(As subtle as a pink elephant tiptoeing in a room filled with really loud bubble wrap!)

However, what is next for you in your persuasion journey?

The answer is pretty simple – go out and do it!

The first key to getting more people to buy your products and services or to do whatever it is you would like them to do is to get out there and actually speak to people. This is THE best thing that you can improve on today, and one that will skyrocket your results.

This is why I started the book with a chapter on how important this principle is. I taught my sales trainee this when I first started, and he taught it back to me when he became the number 1 sales person in the UK – just one week after I taught him the principle!

The cool thing is now you have the advantage of having these skills at your fingertips when you go out and speak to people. You have a lot more potential for persuasion – however, just like a sports car has potential for speed, it does nothing if you leave it parked in the garage.
It's time for you to discover how these different strategies work for you by testing them out.

As with any new skill, it will take some practice for you to fluidly embed these principles into your conversations so that they come out naturally at the right time.

Until then it's a little bit like learning how to cook a new dish, you have to prepare, think it through a little, refer to notes and the first couple of times it may not turn out right. However, with enough practice you can be doing this blindfolded**!

**(Yes, speaking blindfolded is not that difficult, but I was obviously referring to the cooking part.)

When you start, you will find some principles work extremely well with certain individuals and not so well with others. It doesn't mean the principles don't work, it just means that the particular principle you have tried may not work that well on the person you have spoken to (or you may need to tweak your delivery).

For example, I have at times used the principle of "other people's perceptions" and said to people, "the reason people in your area are taking up the offer…" to which they would reply, "I am not really interested in what other people do".

Yes, you get those people!

However, this is where the other 5 principles come into play! People may be more inclined to one or two of the principles versus other principles. When I first heard the above example I would stumble, but after some practice I would be able to seamlessly reply using the other principles of persuasion and say something along the lines of, "Yes, of course, I prefer to make my own decisions too. At the end of the day – ultimately, if you qualify - it is completely your choice if you do this or not. The reason I am here today is to give people who qualify a final chance to do this before the offer is removed."

In a phrase like that I have started with Likeability by relating to the person ("I prefer to make my own decisions too"), created some fear of loss ("if you qualify"), showed some indifference ("It is completely your choice if you do this or not") and finally created further fear of loss ("I am here today, people that qualify, final chance").

Now, the above statement was something relevant and true to the type of service I was offering at the time. You would need to find ways to create statements that relate to your product, service or outcome. I would not recommend using that statement if it is not relevant to you. Having integrity is a key part in persuasion and you don't want to lie just so that you can use the statements.

The key to using the principle of persuasion effectively in your conversation, is to design your offer beforehand so that they already contain the principles of persuasion where relevant. Create a limited number of your product, or if it is a service mention that your time is limited in order to create a fear of loss. Be aware of the selling points of your product to create value, make a note of previous customers in order to push the principle of "other people's perceptions" or perhaps you can give a free trial upfront in order to create the desire for "reciprocity". Doing this allows your conversations to be truthful and naturally contain the principles of persuasion.

To give you a specific example - if you are a therapist, develop a list of people that you will not work with – the mentally ill, those on extreme medication, children under the age of 15, people that have been sent against their own free will – that way, when you talk about having someone qualify before you can work with them, you are being honest.

Or perhaps offer a 5% discount for people that sign up with you on the day that you speak with them. That way, when you talk about the offer being available for today only, you are being truthful.

By crafting your offer to contain principles of persuasion in it, and starting to use these principles in your frequent conversations and interactions, you will gradually improve until you have near superhero like abilities...

...you probably won't be a cat whisperer though, that is reserved for us "special" few....

Just remember, no matter how good you are, always appreciate that there are some people that you just may not have any luck with, like my auntie Fatima... and occasionally, my wife!

But if you have improved your sales or conversions by two, three or four times what they are now that doesn't matter - just sit back and enjoy Auntie Fatima's food!

End.

This book has talked through the principles and subconscious motivators that move people towards taking action. To take your persuasion to the next level consider combining these principles with actual language patterns and questioning techniques designed to move people towards saying "Yes" to you.

As I appreciate you being a reader of my book, I am offering a special discount on my video course "Getting the Yes", designed to teach you the language patterns and questioning techniques that move a person towards taking action. That way, you not only know what concepts to use but also what to say in order to make your influence invincible.

Click here to get more information:

www.muneer.com/persuasion-oto1/

To your continued success,

Muneer

ABOUT THE AUTHOR

Muneer Al Busaidi is an international Amazon best-selling author, a hypnotist, marketer and ex door-to-door salesman.

Starting out as the unpopular and bullied kid - he now speaks, writes, coaches and films all around the world on all things influence, persuasion and client acquisition. To date he has spoken in over 10 countries and continues to speak and film globally.

Over the last 15 years, he has worked with over a thousand people, from sales executives and marketers to trainers and coaches, and has helped them to confidently connect and convert people into taking action.

As a result, businesses he has worked with have generated millions of dollars, relationships have improved (or started) and the people he has worked with have become more confident in approaching others.

Using his vast experience in persuasion-based roles along with his study of NLP, hypnosis and the science gained from his vast research into the subject, Muneer has developed a system using cutting edge stealth tactics to make your influence invincible, and is passionate about helping you become the charismatic person that can connect with anyone and get them to do what you want.

His mission is to touch the lives of 3,000,000 people through his courses, books, videos, podcasts and content.

In the past Muneer has been named Bahrain's funniest person, one of the top 10 arab's on twitter and "a special boy" by his teachers (he still isnt sure if the context was good on the last one).

On Muneer's Youtube channel - he interviews world champions, best selling authors and people with exceptional stories along with inspirational and persuasion videos filmed around the world.

Connect with Muneer Al Busaidi online!

Website: Muneer.com

YouTube: http://www.YouTube.com/Muneer

Facebook: http://www.Facebook.com/MuneerDotCom

Twitter: http://www.Twitter.com/Muneer

Instagram: https://www.instagram.com/muneer.b

Blog: http://www.Muneer.com

Amazon Author Page: http://www.Amazon.com/author/muneer

PRODUCTS BY MUNEER AL BUSAIDI

The Client Creation Formula:

A system to find and convert your ideal client. Save time by automating a list generation through the internet.

Learn more and get my FREE ebook: 21 Places to find your ideal client
http://www.muneer.com/21-places-to-find-coaching-clients/

The Mighty Mindset

A methodology using exercises and videos to design your dream life and become a person that consistently achieves goals and desires.

Learn more and get the video series: The 3 most important steps you can apply today to achieve your goals and your dream life
http://www.muneer.com/mindsetgift/

Invincible Influence

A system to confidently connect, converse and convert the people you meet from prospects to clients.

Learn more and get my FREE guide – 11 Hypnotic Power words of Persuasion: Discover hypnosis hot words that you can start using in the next 47 minutes to make your everyday communication more persuasive

http://www.muneer.com/powerwords/

HIRE MUNEER TO SPEAK AT YOUR EVENT!

Book Muneer Al Busaidi as your Keynote Speaker and You're Guaranteed to Make Your Event Highly Entertaining and Unforgettable!

Over the last decade, Muneer Al Busaidi has been educating, entertaining and speaking around the world. An accomplished speaker, comedian and authority on all things influence, persuasion and client acquisition – to date Muneer has spoken in over 10 countries.

His experience in transforming himself from the unpopular and bullied kid to becoming a master of persuasion who meets with some of the worlds leading experts on influence, hypnosis and communication.
Muneer can share relevant, actionable strategies that anyone can use - even if they're starting from scratch.

Muneer has a fast growing Youtube channel where he currently releases weekly videos and interviews with world champions, and people with exceptional backgrounds.

His unique style inspires, empowers and entertains audiences while giving them the tools and strategies they need to confidently connect, converse and convert prospects into clients.

For more info, visit http://www.muneer.com/speaker/

ONE LAST THING...

If you enjoyed this book or found it useful I'd be very grateful if you'd post a short review on Amazon. Your support really does make a difference and I read all the reviews personally so I can get your feedback and make this book even better.

If you'd like to leave a review then all you need to do is click the review link on this book's page on Amazon here:

https://www.amazon.com/dp/B072R1RVK6

Thanks again for your support!